GW00692177

RETURN TO ME WITH ALL YOUR HEART

RETURN TO ME WITH ALL YOUR HEART
Daily Reflections for Lent

Gerard Gallagher

VERITAS

Published 2020 by
Veritas Publications
7–8 Lower Abbey Street
Dublin 1
Ireland
www.veritas.ie

ISBN 978 1 84730 951 8

Copyright © Gerard Gallagher, 2020

10 9 8 7 6 5 4 3 2 1

A catalogue record for this book is available from the British Library.

Designed by Jeannie Swan, Veritas Publications
Printed in the Republic of Ireland by SPRINT-print Ltd, Dublin

Veritas books are printed on paper made from the wood pulp of
managed forests. For every tree felled, at least one tree is planted,
thereby renewing natural resources.

CONTENTS

INTRODUCTION TO LENT

'He is in you, he is with you and he never abandons you.
However far you may wander, he is always there, the Risen One.'
(POPE FRANCIS)

We all have different memories of Lent. Some of us may feel nostalgic for the holy days that punctuate the season, beginning with the receiving of the blessed ashes on Ash Wednesday. For many, it is the school-yard conversations of 'What are you giving up for Lent?' Others might associate Lent with the Trócaire box and the shadow it cast over the house throughout the forty days of the season. Then there was the sense of reawakening with the commencement of Holy Week.

Times have changed. While there are still residues of popular traditions, it is now more of a challenge for Christians to follow the season of Lent as the cultural supports have fallen away. Nonetheless, for many it remains an opportunity to reflect, to take stock and to examine the core elements of faith.

Lent is a time to begin again, a time to reflect on the life, death and Resurrection of Jesus Christ. It is a time for each of us to reflect on this personal relationship and in ways allow space for it to deepen. There is time still in your personal life to recapture the sense of what Lent is. Lent is connected to Easter and Pentecost. But the journey begins with one important step on Ash Wednesday.

The goal of this book is to help you to reflect, to pray and to deepen your personal relationship with Jesus Christ. It is comprised of extracts from scripture, the inspiring words of various saints and venerable figures from the Church and my own reflections. Some days might be more relevant to you

than others. The important thing is to stick with the task. If you want a deeper relationship with Jesus, contemplation, prayer and commitment are essential. You are free to pick and choose. The key is that you face the direction of Jesus and begin your pilgrim path towards his glory.

Decide on a particular time of day during which you will begin your daily prayer, be it morning, afternoon or evening. Choose a quiet, comfortable space that is conducive to prayer. Begin by taking a moment to unwind, preferably in silence. However, if you are not fully comfortable with silence, choose some reflective instrumental music to play in the background.

Each of the daily reflections can be broken up into three parts:

1. READ a suggested passage from scripture and reflect upon what it might mean to you personally.

2. REFLECT on some of the themes emerging from the daily readings.

3. RESPOND or make an action to try to change or do something differently.

At the end of your prayer, remember to give thanks to God for the time you have spent with him. Try to end with a word that will keep you anchored and that echoes in your mind and with your thoughts. Offer this time to God.

ASH WEDNESDAY
Turn to the Lord

The ashes used on Ash Wednesday are made from the burning of palms blessed in the previous year's Palm Sunday celebration. The ritual is derived from the Gospel accounts of Jesus' path being covered in palm fronds on the day he entered Jerusalem.

READ
Today, slowly read the following passage from scripture and ponder each line carefully

Yet even now, says the Lord,

return to me with all your heart,

with fasting, with weeping, and with mourning;

rend your hearts and not your clothing.

Return to the Lord, your God,

for he is gracious and merciful,

slow to anger, and abounding in steadfast love,

and relents from punishing.

Who knows whether he will not turn and relent,

and leave a blessing behind him,

a grain offering and a drink offering

for the Lord, your God? (Jl 2:12-14)

REFLECT

Lent is a struggle not just between good and evil, but between mercy and love. Lent can teach us a discipline that can help throughout the year. As you begin your journey into Lent, what are your intentions as you are invited to return to the Lord 'with all your heart' (Joel 2:12)? Pope Francis reminds us that there 'are Christians whose lives seem like Lent without Easter.' We need to celebrate Lent with a view to also celebrating Easter.

Lent is time set aside for all Christians to reflect and encounter Jesus. Lent is not a season to be morbid, but a time for all followers to reconsider their relationship with Christ who suffered, died and subsequently fulfilled his promise of giving us eternal life through the Resurrection. Prepare yourself to encounter some of the people who accompanied Jesus on this journey. There will be times when we might identify with some of the supporters of Jesus and some of those who denied Jesus too.

Today's Gospel reminds us of the three core tenets of Lent: to give, to pray and to fast. Through three actions, we will find our reward.

RESPOND

• During this season of Lent, how do you plan to give, pray and fast in ways that will bring you into a deeper relationship with Christ?

• How do you plan to set your compass and direct your life towards that of Christ?

THURSDAY AFTER ASH WEDNESDAY

'Yet all is not lost. Human beings, while capable of the worst,
are also capable of rising above themselves, choosing again
what is good, and making a new start ...'

POPE FRANCIS

READ

Today, slowly read the following passage from scripture and ponder each line carefully
See, I have set before you today life and prosperity, death
and adversity. If you obey the commandments of the Lord
your God that I am commanding you today, by loving the
Lord your God, walking in his ways, and observing his
commandments, decrees, and ordinances, then you shall live
and become numerous, and the Lord your God will bless you
in the land that you are entering to possess. But if your heart
turns away and you do not hear, but are led astray to bow
down to other gods and serve them, I declare to you today
that you shall perish; you shall not live long in the land that
you are crossing the Jordan to enter and possess. I call heaven
and earth to witness against you today that I have set before
you life and death, blessings and curses. Choose life so that
you and your descendants may live, loving the Lord your
God... (Deut 30:15-20)

REFLECT

Today we invite the Lord to help us begin again and to continue
with his help as we take another step on our lenten journey.
Following God is not easy. It is the road less travelled.
Sometimes it can be easier to give up, go with the flow or just
copy what other people do. Sometimes it is easier just to think

of oneself rather than others. Sometimes it might be easier to reject God as it might make our life and work easier. God has given us commandments. Some of these became laws and customs. If we try to walk his path – to love our neighbour and family – then we will remain on the path towards God. There is more to life than merely feeling that we simply exist. Being on God's path can help us to live a new life with fullness (Jn 10:10). Ultimately true happiness and contentment can be found by reflecting on our relationship with God. 'Happy the one who has placed his trust in the Lord' (Ps 1:1). Jesus explains that if we are to follow the path in his direction, we must also carry his cross. To 'like' Jesus is not the same as liking or following something on social media. To like Jesus has consequences and implications. It is not a passive click on your phone to 'like' him. To like Jesus means paying attention to his words and deeds. It's part of the deal. Jesus becomes the filter through which we perceive the world. 'If anyone wants to be a follower of mine, let him renounce himself and take up his cross every day' (Lk 9:23).

RESPOND

• Reflect on times in your life when you have placed your trust in God and consider what happened next?

• Have you ever rejected the 'love' of God for other loves because it was easier?

• If you 'follow' Jesus, what does this mean practically for you?

• How can you follow Jesus this day?

FRIDAY AFTER ASH WEDNESDAY

'The Lord heard me and took pity on me. He came to my help.'
ENTRANCE ANTIPHON

*'As we approach the season of Lent ... these days should
be given to fasting. This means not just reducing food which
benefits soul and body, but the elimination of unworthy habits.'*
POPE LEO THE GREAT

READ

Today, slowly read the following passage from scripture and ponder each line carefully.
Then the disciples of John came to him, saying, 'Why do we
and the Pharisees fast often, but your disciples do not fast?'
And Jesus said to them, 'The wedding guests cannot mourn if
the bridegroom is with them, can they? The days will come
when the bridegroom is taken away from them, and then
they will fast.' (Mt 9:14-15)

REFLECT

Fasting is one of the traditions of Lent that has been passed on
from generation to generation. Fasting, unlike dieting, is not
something to be taken up for personal benefit. Isaiah raises
the question about the type of fasting that we undertake. 'Is
not this the sort of fast that pleases?' (Is 58:1-9) Jesus reminds
us that if we fast, we really should not do so in a morose
fashion but with a sense of gratitude, even joy. The focus here
is on building a personal relationship with God. The hunger
and the denial which are part and parcel of fasting are an
invitation to follow Jesus on the path towards his passion,
death and Resurrection. If it is carried out with discretion,

God will notice and reward you with the promise of a better life to come.

RESPOND

• If you decide to fast today, what foods will you choose to forgo?

• If you are hungry as a result, how do you connect this experience to your relationship with God?

• As you fast from food or forgo another pleasure, what do you choose to replace the experience with?

• Can you fast enough for one day to really experience hunger?

SATURDAY AFTER ASH WEDNESDAY

'Some people at first may be hard hearted and persist in sin
but then God, in his mercy, allows them to be afflicted. Then
they grow weary of their ways, come to their senses and are
converted. They draw near to God and come to knowledge,
repent wholeheartedly, and attain the true way of life.'

ST ANTONY OF EGYPT

READ

Today, slowly read the following passage from scripture and ponder each line carefully

After this he went out and saw a tax collector named Levi,
sitting at the tax booth; and he said to him, 'Follow me.' And
he got up, left everything, and followed him.

Then Levi gave a great banquet for him in his house; and
there was a large crowd of tax collectors and others sitting
at the table with them. The Pharisees and their scribes were
complaining to his disciples, saying, 'Why do you eat and
drink with tax collectors and sinners?' Jesus answered, 'Those
who are well have no need of a physician, but those who
are sick; I have come to call not the righteous but sinners to
repentance.' (Lk 5:27-32)

REFLECT

How many times have we failed to pick up on something
that's actually very significant and only discover as much at a
later date? It is only through moments of contemplation or
reflection that we realise we missed some important detail.
Think of some of the great television dramas or films. The
final reveal often involves details or elements that were so
obvious in retrospect.

We are told that Jesus 'noticed a tax collector, Levi by name'. The gaze of Jesus was also matched by his ability to know everyone by name. He called people by their name. Jesus noticed those who were with him. More importantly he noticed the people on the periphery. Jesus' mercy went beyond those who followed him. Jesus invited Levi to do the unthinkable, to follow him. Matthew's Gospel tells us, 'God never tires of forgiving us, we are the ones who tire of seeking his mercy' (Mt 18:22). God does not disappoint. Anyone who follows the word of God, the person of Jesus and the mission given to him will know one fact: our mission will not disappoint.

RESPOND
• Try to notice the people that you encounter as you go about your business today. If you get a chance greet them by name and take a moment to speak with them, listening carefully to what they have to say.

• Just like Levi, you have been called by Jesus. Take a moment during the day to reflect on what it means to you to be a follower of Jesus today in your world.

• Is there someone in your life that needs mercy? Are you prepared to take a risk like Levi and leave your old life behind in order to redirect your gaze towards Jesus?

FIRST WEEK OF LENT

SUNDAY

'Lent stimulates us to let the Word of God penetrate our life and in this way to know the fundamental truth: who we are, where we come from, where we must go, what path we must take in life ...'

POPE BENEDICT XVI

READ

Today, slowly read the following passage from scripture and ponder each line carefully

For if the many died through the one man's trespass, much more surely have the grace of God and the free gift in the grace of the one man, Jesus Christ, abounded for the many. And the free gift is not like the effect of the one man's sin. For the judgement following one trespass brought condemnation, but the free gift following many trespasses brings justification. If, because of the one man's trespass, death exercised dominion through that one, much more surely will those who receive the abundance of grace and the free gift of righteousness exercise dominion in life through the one man, Jesus Christ. (Rm 5:14-18)

REFLECT

During this first week of Lent we try to keep our focus on what type of journey we are embarking on. It is a time to recall who this person called Jesus was and what he did out of love for each one of us. He was God's plan. His plan also has a place for us. To reflect and enter onto the path Jesus took towards Jerusalem can bring many rewards and challenges. Lent is not an easy path. Our readings reflect stories of temptation and difficult decisions that must be made. We can

all be tempted to cut corners in our daily lives. We can justify every slip in our choices. Jesus was tempted daily for forty days; we will be tempted too. Lent is a journey in discovering ourselves. However, it is not a selfish journey. It needs to be selfless like Jesus. If we can try to make Jesus' words and deeds our own that will be a good start. If we can also try to keep our focus on this path to Jerusalem, our lenten journey will be an adventure into our faith and personal relationship with Jesus. Whatever your intentions this Lent, know that you are not alone. There are other people in many parts of the world embarking on this journey. Keep in mind that in our observance of the first week of Lent the light of Jesus' death and Resurrection will be our guide. Our ultimate challenge is how to reflect this in our daily lives.

RESPOND

• What choices have I made this Lent to try to become closer to Jesus?

• What actions in my personal life will change as a result of my lenten experiences this year?

MONDAY

'It is your life that Jesus wants to enter with his word, with his presence. Please, let Christ and his word enter your life, blossom and grow.'

POPE FRANCIS

READ

Today, slowly read the following passage from scripture and ponder each line carefully

The Lord spoke to Moses, saying: 'Speak to all the congregation of the people of Israel and say to them: You shall be holy, for I the Lord your God am holy. You shall not steal; you shall not deal falsely; and you shall not lie to one another. And you shall not swear falsely by my name, profaning the name of your God: I am the Lord.

'You shall not defraud your neighbour; you shall not steal; and you shall not keep for yourself the wages of a labourer until morning. You shall not revile the deaf or put a stumbling block before the blind; you shall fear your God: I am the Lord.' (Lev 19:1-2; 11-14)

REFLECT

If you truly want to get closer to God in your life this Lent one method is to begin to get closer to yourself. Bookshops are full of self-help publications. We are surrounded by people who spend lots of time on their phone updating their social media accounts. Our lives are meant to be more than just a parody on social media. Getting to know God more during Lent begins by recognising we need to direct our attention towards the divine rather than the online.

We are reminded today in God's word that 'our eyes are fixed on the Lord'. There are many distractions in our world, and it can be hard to remain focused on the Lord. However, this is our challenge to live the spiritual life in a secular context. There is a call to be holy and live Lent in a holy way. God speaking to Moses reminded him to 'be holy'. Holiness comes with a challenge. To try to be holy means not acting like everyone else. Your challenge is reimagining yourself as a holy person trying to love your neighbour as much as you love yourself. As you walk this path of Lent on this first Monday you are encountering yourself at a crossroads. You can choose any direction. However, your invitation is to follow the path that leads towards God.

RESPOND

• Today, take some time to speak with those whom you meet. What do you notice about these conversations?

• Do your actions bring you closer to God or are you finding yourself struggling to 'love your neighbour'?

• If you were able to adjust one aspect of your life, what would it be?

• Do you ever make time to reflect on your life?

TUESDAY
'Through the discipline of Lent help us to grow in our desire for you.'
OPENING PRAYER

'After going into the chapel, I place myself in the presence of God and I say to Him, "Lord here I am: give me whatever you wish." '
ST CATHERINE LABOURÉ

READ

Today, slowly read the following passage from scripture and ponder each line carefully

Pray then in this way:

Our Father in heaven,
hallowed be your name.
Your kingdom come.
Your will be done,
on earth as it is in heaven.
Give us this day our daily bread.
And forgive us our debts,
as we also have forgiven our debtors.
And do not bring us to the time of trial,
but rescue us from the evil one.

For if you forgive others their trespasses, your heavenly Father will also forgive you; but if you do not forgive others, neither will your Father forgive your trespasses. (Mt 6:9-15)

REFLECT

I have only met a few people who say prayer is easy for them. I meet many people who struggle to find either the words for prayer or the right moment. The desire for prayer is an ancient echo. Generations before us have integrated prayer into their daily lives. The rhythm of the monastery bell and the call to prayer is as strong as the person who sits in a church in the silence, just contemplating. The parent with small noisy children in church struggles to pray, especially with all the mature people watching and judging. I have met people who pray as they walk, run or just sit in their favourite chair at home. Prayer is one of the most accessible forms of connecting with and encountering yourself in the presence of God. No matter what your state of mind, God is ready for you and your prayer. Prayer is a dialogue, not a monologue. During this first week of Lent, prepare to go on a journey and make a regular time to pray, contemplate and nurture your lenten journey. Try the 'Our Father' to start; it is where Jesus began after all.

RESPOND

• Are you happy with your prayer life? How could you improve it?

• Prayer is personal and something that is shared. What is the focus of your prayers?

• Read the 'Our Father' slowly. Pause on some of the words and really let them sink in ... what do you notice about your prayer?

WEDNESDAY

'Let us not allow this season of grace to pass in vain! Let us ask
God to help us set out on a path of true conversion ...
Let us stand beside our brothers and sisters in need,
sharing our spiritual and material goods with them.'

POPE FRANCIS

READ

Today, slowly read the following passage from scripture and ponder each line carefully
The word of the Lord came to Jonah a second time, saying,
'Get up, go to Nineveh, that great city, and proclaim to it
the message that I tell you.' So, Jonah set out and went to
Nineveh, according to the word of the Lord. Now Nineveh
was an exceedingly large city, a three-day walk across. Jonah
began to go into the city, going a day's walk. And he cried
out, 'Forty days more, and Nineveh shall be overthrown!' And
the people of Nineveh believed God; they proclaimed a fast,
and everyone, great and small, put on sackcloth.

When God saw what they did, how they turned from their
evil ways, God changed his mind about the calamity that he
had said he would bring upon them; and he did not do it.
(Jon 3:1-5, 10)

REFLECT

Now that you have completed the first week of Lent, it is a
good time to reflect on how your time walking this lenten
path has been for you. You might find yourself distracted or
tempted to fall into previous patterns of life. You might notice
a new rhythm or strength. Today in our reading we encounter
Jonah. We are told that the 'word of God was addressed' to

him. God's word is indeed personal. For Jonah it required a response. It required him to do something almost impossible. Jonah's task was to do as God said and to remind the people of Nineveh that they needed to redirect their lives towards God, by being humbler, to repent and fast. We are told the people responded. Imagine if you were Jonah – how would you respond to such a seemingly impossible task? Remember everything is possible for those who listen and follow God's word. The invitation today is for you to listen more closely to God's word and then to do as Jonah did, to get up and go and respond. Our Christian history is full of many great humble people who did mighty deeds, just because they listened to God and responded to the best of their ability. Everyone is called by God. God can do the impossible in each of our lives.

RESPOND

- Spend some time today imagining that God has called you to do one thing. How would you respond?
- Can you recall a time you felt really called or inspired to do something that had a positive impact on others?
- Have you tried letting go?

THURSDAY

'Lord make me a channel of your peace. Where there is
hatred let me bring your love: where there is injury
your pardon, where there is doubt, true faith in you.'

ST FRANCIS OF ASSISI

READ

Today, slowly read the following passage from scripture and ponder each line carefully
Ask, and it will be given to you; search, and you will find;
knock, and the door will be opened for you. For everyone
who asks receives, and everyone who searches finds, and
for everyone who knocks, the door will be opened. Is there
anyone among you who, if your child asks for bread, will
give a stone? Or if the child asks for a fish, will give a snake? If
you then, who are evil, know how to give good gifts to your
children, how much more will your Father in heaven give
good things to those who ask him! (Mt 7:8-10)

REFLECT

In the Old Testament, Esther took refuge in the Lord when she
found herself in 'peril'. Her last option was to turn to God.
In society today we have a greater awareness than ever before
that some people have days when they see no hope. Many
have to contend with mental illness, depression or thoughts
of despair on a daily basis. There are myriad reasons why
people succumb to despair, be it because of financial woes,
the loss of a loved one or any number of personal setbacks.
At some point everyone has been in the position where a
'peril' in their life has led them to encounter the Lord. There
are times where we all cry 'out of the depths' to the Lord

who alone has the compassionate response. Jesus made it clear to his disciples that the one who asks, always receives. Sometimes we can be impatient and implore the Lord to answer in our time. However, God's time and response might not be what we are expecting. This, of course, is the God who invited us all to 'come back to me with all your heart'. Today, reach out to those who might be experiencing difficulty and try to offer the compassionate word or gesture; this in turn might 'give again the joy of your help.'

RESPOND

• Think of the times when you felt the whole weight of the world was on your shoulders. How did you get through that experience? What gave you the courage?

• Think of friends or loved ones who are going through a tough time in life. In what ways can you offer them practical support?

• In your prayers remember the many who are in 'peril' and especially those who are persecuted for their faith.

FRIDAY

'If I am not in God's grace, may God bring me there;
If I am in it, may He keep me there.'

ST JOAN OF ARC

'Act in such a way that all those who come in contact with
you will go away joyful. Sow happiness about you
because you have received much from God'.

ST FAUSTINA

READ

Today, slowly read the following passage from scripture and ponder each line carefully

But if the wicked turn away from all their sins that they have committed and keep all my statutes and do what is lawful and right, they shall surely live; they shall not die. None of the transgressions that they have committed shall be remembered against them; for the righteousness that they have done they shall live. Have I any pleasure in the death of the wicked, says the Lord God, and not rather that they should turn from their ways and live?

But when the righteous turn away from their righteousness and commit iniquity and do the same abominable things that the wicked do, shall they live? None of the righteous deeds that they have done shall be remembered; for the treachery of which they are guilty and the sin they have committed, they shall die. (Ez 18:21-24)

REFLECT

Fridays have traditionally been days when pilgrims focus on reconciliation. Jesus did say that no one can come to the

father without being reconciled. Creating good relations with everyone in life is important. We live in a world where there are people that are regularly subject to abuse. Some people think they can use social media to demean others, particularly those of another faith or ethnicity. Being able to reflect on the difference I can make in my world can help me reflect on the impact I have on the people that I need to reconcile with. Reflecting on those times you may have engaged in gossip or ridiculed another human being is important when it comes to understanding whether you are more a scribe or a Pharisee. We need to take up the invitation and embrace a new heart and a new spirit in everything that we do.

RESPOND
• Can I think of anyone in my life that I need to be reconciled with? Am I ready to be reconciled with that person?
• Am I someone who asks for forgiveness?

SATURDAY

*'Turn our hearts to you. By seeking your kingdom
and loving one another ... may we become a people who
worship you in spirit and truth.'*
OPENING PRAYER

*'Did I offer peace today? Did I bring a smile to
someone's face? Did I say words of healing?
Did I let go of my anger and resentment?
Did I forgive? Did I love? These are real questions.'*
HENRI NOUWEN

READ

Today, slowly read the following passage from scripture and ponder each line carefully

This very day the Lord your God is commanding you to observe these statutes and ordinances; so observe them diligently with all your heart and with all your soul.

Today you have obtained the Lord's agreement: to be your God; and for you to walk in his ways, to keep his statutes, his commandments, and his ordinances, and to obey him. Today the Lord has obtained your agreement: to be his treasured people, as he promised you, and to keep his commandments; for him to set you high above all nations that he has made, in praise and in fame and in honour; and for you to be a people holy to the Lord your God, as he promised. (Deut 26:16-19)

REFLECT

Every new community needs some guidance or laws. We live in a society where there are many public policies and statutes to guide every aspect of life. The Israelites were given very

clear direction from Moses that God's law was paramount. Moses did not say try and follow as many as you can. If we are a member of a club or society, then the rules are what sets us apart. Golf clubs are not venues where rugby takes place; we don't play tennis with hockey sticks. There are rules. Being Christian also means following a way that sets us apart. The early Christians understood this. Many became martyrs as they tried to remain true to their new faith at all costs. When we stand for something, we can receive respect for this. Often people look to Jesus and say: 'We like him, his message, but it's not for me.' There are others who follow Christ but lead lives that are not Christian. Today each of us is invited to reflect on how these rules of love that were given by God both to test us and to bring us closer to him are expressed in our lives. We can become more like Christ if we try to follow him in his words and deeds. It is not easy to follow the law and the customs of faith. However, God invites us today to persevere.

RESPOND

• Looking at your life, what areas of your life are you pleased with?

• Have you ever tried to 'pray for those who persecute' you or other people? We can recall the thief on the cross next to Jesus or even St Paul who was one of the great persecutors but changed to be a follower.

• Do you pick and choose some of the laws of God rather than being a true follower?

SECOND WEEK OF LENT

SUNDAY

'God has created me to do Him some definite service; He has committed some work to me which he has not committed to another. I have my mission. I may never know it in this life but I shall be told it in the next. I am a link in a chain, a bond of connection between persons. He has not created me for naught. I shall do good, I shall do His work; shall be an angel of peace, a preacher of truth in my own place, while not intending it, if I do but keep His commandments.'

ST JOHN HENRY NEWMAN

READ

Today, slowly read the following passage from scripture and ponder each line carefully

While he was still speaking, suddenly a bright cloud overshadowed them, and from the cloud a voice said, 'This is my Son, the Beloved; with him I am well pleased; listen to him!' When the disciples heard this, they fell to the ground and were overcome by fear. But Jesus came and touched them, saying, 'Get up and do not be afraid.' And when they looked up, they saw no one except Jesus himself alone. As they were coming down the mountain, Jesus ordered them, 'Tell no one about the vision until after the Son of Man has been raised from the dead.' (Mt 17:5-9)

REFLECT

God has a unique plan for each of us. Our progress this Lent includes reflecting on this mystery of what our purpose is. Finding your purpose is key to finding out who you really are. Some people have achieved this greatness by design or by accident. Discerning what plan God has for each of us requires paying attention to every detail. Abram was told that he was

not only going to be great, but he would be remembered as a blessing. Each of us can become a blessing for another person. If we can really trust in God and place all our hope in God, then only God knows what our future holds. Our encounter with God is both a mystery and a privilege. Just like the disciples who encountered Jesus in a new way on the mountain, their initial reaction was to 'stay'. Just as things were beginning to fall into place for them, the encounter with Jesus involved getting off the mountain. It would be a while before they would be ready to speak about their encounter. Lent is a time to wait with the Lord. A time to be open to new encounters with God. It is also a time to prepare for future and unexpected encounters with God. God knows your purpose and knows when you are ready. You might not be ready to tell people about what your relationship with God is like. However, the right time will come.

RESPOND

• How do I 'listen' to God in my life? Do I really know what I am called to do?

• Look at some of the great followers of Jesus. Did you ever notice how many of them felt inadequate when faced with the call of God but allowed God's purpose to become their purpose? What is your purpose in life?

MONDAY

'I urgently appeal then for a new dialogue about how we are shaping the future of our planet. We need a conversation which includes everyone, since the environmental challenge we are undergoing, and its human roots, concern and affect us all.'

POPE FRANCIS

READ

Today, slowly read the following passage from scripture and ponder each line carefully

O God, the nations have come into your inheritance;
  they have defiled your holy temple;
  they have laid Jerusalem in ruins.
They have given the bodies of your servants
  to the birds of the air for food,
  the flesh of your faithful to the wild animals of the earth.
They have poured out their blood like water
  all around Jerusalem,
  and there was no one to bury them.
We have become a taunt to our neighbours,
  mocked and derided by those around us.
Do not remember against us the iniquities of our ancestors;
  let your compassion come speedily to meet us,
  for we are brought very low.

(Ps 79:1-4, 8)

REFLECT

There is a general consensus now that all of us have a role to play in 'shaping the future of our planet' and that humanity has failed to care for our 'common home'. Rampant

consumerism, the depletion of natural resources, pollution and the destruction of ecosystems has had a detrimental impact on the food chain and on the planet. We have abused our Garden of Eden. There is hope, however, if we respond in meaningful and urgent ways. Our children and inspirational young people like Greta Thunberg are very much crusaders when it comes to awareness around the environment. Our communities of believers can work together to accomplish change in local areas. We need new coalitions of the willing who wish to try to save our planet for future generations. The Psalmist cries: 'Do not hold the guilt of our fathers against us.' Their cry is for help, not for judgement.

RESPOND

• Pope Francis has asked: 'What kind of world do we want to leave to those who come after us, to children who are now growing up?' Spend a few moments answering this question.
• During these days of Lent what are the personal changes you can make to the world that you live in, especially if you believe every person can make a difference?

TUESDAY

'To know Christ is know God. Christ is the homily that keeps explaining to us continually that God is love, that God is power, that the Spirit of the Lord is upon Jesus Christ, that he is the divine Word, God's presence among us.'

ÓSCAR ROMERO

'Learn to do good, search for justice, help the oppressed.'

ISAIAH 1:10

READ

Today, slowly read the following passage from scripture and ponder each line carefully

Wash yourselves; make yourselves clean;
   remove the evil of your doings
   from before my eyes;
cease to do evil,
   learn to do good;
seek justice,
   rescue the oppressed,
defend the orphan,
   plead for the widow.

Come now, let us argue it out,
   says the Lord:
though your sins are like scarlet,
   they shall be like snow;
though they are red like crimson,
   they shall become like wool.
If you are willing and obedient,
   you shall eat the good of the land;

but if you refuse and rebel,
  you shall be devoured by the sword;
  for the mouth of the Lord has spoken.

(Is 1:16-20)

REFLECT

We are citizens of this world and are governed by the laws of many different lands. Most modern laws have been handed down and evolved over the centuries into various forms of code. The commandments given to the Israelites are still followed today. Jesus came not to change the law but to enhance it in the Gospel of 'love one another'. Irrespective of where you live − in the Western 'modern' world, or in a young democracy or in a land where Christians are a minority − we are all called to follow the commandments and teachings of our faith. At times this has led followers of Jesus into direct conflict with the local laws and customs. Our Christian history is made up of martyrs who shed their blood in defence of their faith. Ireland has its martyrs from the penal times. There are also prophets of the modern era such as Óscar Romero or Jerzy Popiełuszko. These are just two people from the twentieth century who experienced epiphanies and chose to stand up for God, and live out the Gospels even if it meant losing their lives. Both these people have followed the first Christians and were humbled by listening to the cry of the people. It is still our duty to bring the Gospel message to our world in difficult times. However, history is still being repeated today in the Holy Lands of the Middle East where minorities continue to suffer. Many are escaping to new lands. The Exodus from oppression continues to this day.

RESPOND

• Have you ever listened to the stories of the new people who live in our communities?

• Many families have members who left to travel to foreign lands where it becomes challenging to live their faith. Have you ever reached out to them with a compassionate word?

WEDNESDAY

'When a leader allows himself to succumb to the wishes of those he leads, of those who will always seek to turn him into their idol, the image of the leader will gradually become the image of the "miss-leader"... This is the leader who makes an idol of himself and his office, and who thus mocks God!'

DIETRICH BONHOEFFER

READ

Today, slowly read the following passage from scripture and ponder each line carefully

Then they said, 'Come, let us make plots against Jeremiah – for instruction shall not perish from the priest, nor counsel from the wise, nor the word from the prophet. Come, let us bring charges against him, and let us not heed any of his words.'

Give heed to me, O Lord,
and listen to what my adversaries say!
Is evil a recompense for good?
Yet they have dug a pit for my life.
Remember how I stood before you
to speak good for them,
to turn away your wrath from them. (Jer 18:18-20)

REFLECT

There are countless examples in history of people whose formerly illustrious careers ended in abject failure and disgrace. Even in the Church today we have instances of once formidable Church leaders who have been imprisoned for wrongdoing. Jesus knew the shadow of the cross that was inching towards him. For Jeremiah, a plot unfolded to 'let us hit him' and damage him. Jesus was aware of the rumblings of discontent that were happening around him. In a way he was preparing his followers for the days that lay ahead. However, they failed to understand or accept what was happening. Their denial also led to their regrets and remorse in the days that followed the Passover and the handing over of Jesus to his persecutors. The Apostles' tendency to jostle for the position of being Christ's 'successor' was rebuked by Jesus when he told them that they needed to be 'servants' of his word, not his heirs. Popularity is a precarious accolade. In modern time social media and pop culture create heroes overnight, but destroy them just as promptly. While we might be 'entertained' by the experience, we are desensitised now to the personal and human wreckage that is left once the media moves on. Jesus' message is for us to be cautious towards those awarded 'hero' status in our society. He is reminding us that we all need to experience the shadow of the cross and the attendant pain and sorrow if we really want to be part of the Resurrection story.

RESPOND

• Who are the prominent personalities and figures in the world that attract you? What are their qualities? Why are they worth following?

• Are you ambitious or have you ever wished to be seen as popular?

THURSDAY

'Dear Jesus, I must admit that I do not see your face in the poor. Sometimes I am so busy with my own concerns that I don't recognise you in that beggar by the side of the road. Help me, dearest Jesus, become more aware of the needs that exist among the needy all around us. Help me share what I have to alleviate their thirst and hunger. Help me show the heart of a loving God, a God who cares for those on the margins.'

POPE FRANCIS

'When we fail to live as children of God, we often behave in a destructive way towards our neighbours.'

POPE FRANCIS

READ

Today, slowly read the following passage from scripture and ponder each line carefully

Thus says the Lord:
'Cursed are those who trust in mere mortals
  and make mere flesh their strength,
  whose hearts turn away from the Lord.
They shall be like a shrub in the desert,
  and shall not see when relief comes.
They shall live in the parched places of the wilderness,
  in an uninhabited salt land.

Blessed are those who trust in the Lord,
  whose trust is the Lord.
They shall be like a tree planted by water,
  sending out its roots by the stream.

It shall not fear when heat comes,
   and its leaves shall stay green;
in the year of drought it is not anxious,
   and it does not cease to bear fruit.' (Jer 17:5-8)

REFLECT

Outside Christ Church Cathedral in Dublin there is a sculpture entitled *Homeless Jesus* which depicts a destitute Christ taking cover under blankets on a park bench. It is very evocative. Though thousands pass it each day, few stop to consider its message. We have all seen homeless people of every creed and colour on our streets seeking help. Sometimes we avert our eyes. We might even cross the street to avoid contact. At this time of great economic prosperity the reality of poverty remains. The divide between rich and poor has been with us since time immemorial. Jesus forces us to reflect on the dichotomy between rich and poor, the contrast between those in power and those on the margins. There is a story told by Pope Francis that on the evening of his election as pope, a cardinal whispered in his ear: 'Don't forget the poor.' This mission statement has been integrated into his papacy. He has chosen to live a simple lifestyle; he has repurposed some of the key Church leaders to reach out to and be with the poor. Poverty is also linked to economic and environmental issues. Jesus points out that during his day the rich were more interested in profits than prophets. People know what they need to do to change. Jesus reminds the disciples that even if 'someone should rise from the dead' they won't change. The next time you see someone who is destitute, reach out to them without judgement. In doing so you are following the example of Christ.

RESPOND
• Lent is about almsgiving; how do you give to the poor?
• Are there other ways that you can identify more with Lazarus than the Rich Man? What changes do you need to make?

FRIDAY

'Lenten practices of giving up pleasures are good reminders
that the purpose of life is not pleasure. The purpose of life is
to attain to perfect life, all truth and undying ecstatic love —
which is the definition of God. In pursuing that goal we find
happiness. Pleasure is not the purpose of anything;
pleasure is a by-product resulting from doing something that is
good. One of the best ways to get happiness and pleasure out of
life is to ask ourselves, "How can I please God?' and,
'Why am I not better?" It is the pleasure-seeker who is
bored, for all pleasures diminish with repetition.'

FULTON J. SHEEN

'The Bible is full of families, births,
love stories and family crises.'

POPE FRANCIS

READ

Today, slowly read the following passage from scripture and ponder each line carefully
Now his brothers went to pasture their father's flock near
Shechem. And Israel said to Joseph, 'Are not your brothers
pasturing the flock at Shechem? Come, I will send you to
them.' He answered, 'Here I am.' So he said to him, 'Go now,
see if it is well with your brothers and with the flock; and
bring word back to me.' So he sent him from the valley of
Hebron.

He came to Shechem, and a man found him wandering in
the fields; the man asked him, 'What are you seeking?' 'I am
seeking my brothers,' he said; 'tell me, please, where they are

pasturing the flock.' The man said, 'They have gone away, for I heard them say, "Let us go to Dothan."'

So Joseph went after his brothers, and found them at Dothan. They saw him from a distance, and before he came near to them, they conspired to kill him. They said to one another, 'Here comes this dreamer. Come now, let us kill him and throw him into one of the pits; then we shall say that a wild animal has devoured him, and we shall see what will become of his dreams.' But when Reuben heard it, he delivered him out of their hands, saying, 'Let us not take his life.' Reuben said to them, 'Shed no blood; throw him into this pit here in the wilderness, but lay no hand on him' that he might rescue him out of their hand and restore him to his father. So when Joseph came to his brothers, they stripped him of his robe, the long robe with sleeves that he wore; and they took him and threw him into a pit. The pit was empty; there was no water in it. (Gn 37:12-24)

REFLECT

I don't think that the perfect family has ever existed. Some have come close. Somewhere in the patterns of family life human frailties emerge. Favouritism, neglect, jealousy, property or position in the family can all lead to various divisions. The experience of young parents raising a family can be both joyous and challenging. Maturing into this relationship and creating a safe home environment where everyone's needs are met has been a cycle of life going back to our origins. I don't think there has ever been an easy time to raise a family. Siblings can and do clash. Siblings can also be each other's best friend and harshest critic. In the Old Testament Joseph was loved by his father and increasingly despised by his brothers.

The mystery of family life is how and why this happens. Another mystery is why some of us stand at the periphery of family life and allow disputes to escalate. Rows can and do happen. A wise piece of counsel for married couples was never to let the sun go down on anger. Make peace at the end of each day. If there is a conflict in your family, try to create the conditions for peace and healing.

RESPOND

• Instead of trying to dig up the past hurts in your family, are there any positive actions you can take to help bring healing?
• What role do you play in your family? Can you improve this?

SATURDAY

'God's mercy embraces those who have disobeyed and those who
have been disappointed. Lent invites us to look at both brothers
to see how they both stand before God in need of mercy,
grace and salvation.'

POPE FRANCIS

'Teach me to be generous, to give and not to count the cost.
To toil and not to seek for rest. To labour and seek no reward,
save of knowing I do your will ... Pray as if everything
depended on God and work as if everything depended on you.'

PRAYER OF ST IGNATIUS

READ

Today, slowly read the following passage from scripture and ponder each line carefully

Now his elder son was in the field; and when he came and
approached the house, he heard music and dancing. He called
one of the slaves and asked what was going on. He replied,
'Your brother has come, and your father has killed the fatted
calf, because he has got him back safe and sound.' Then he
became angry and refused to go in. His father came out and
began to plead with him. But he answered his father, 'Listen!
For all these years I have been working like a slave for you,
and I have never disobeyed your command; yet you have
never given me even a young goat so that I might celebrate
with my friends. But when this son of yours came back, who
has devoured your property with prostitutes, you killed the
fatted calf for him!' Then the father said to him, 'Son, you are
always with me, and all that is mine is yours. But we had to

celebrate and rejoice, because this brother of yours was dead and has come to life; he was lost and has been found.' (Lk 15: 25-31)

REFLECT

The parable of the prodigal son is well known. There have been many interpretations of it. People have commented on it, painted it and used it as an example of God's mercy. One of my favourite interpretations of it is the image of the 'running father'. Parents can relate to this image. No matter what a son or daughter has done to their family, the image of the father running – arms wide open in forgiveness – towards his wayward son is the image that resonates. Parents' hearts have been broken, families destroyed, but the love of a mother or father is greater than all the brokenness. Despite the behaviour of those close to us, we continue to love them. God's compassion is immense. Our sense of despair in life can be offset by the merciful father running towards us to salve our sense of loss. During this day an opportunity might arise to offer forgiveness or ask for mercy. The challenge is not to let it go another day. Be merciful *today* and run towards forgiveness.

RESPOND

• Consider seeking forgiveness for something in your life – God's mercy is immense.

• Try to offer compassion to people you meet today, without judgement or conditions.

THIRD WEEK OF LENT

SUNDAY

'As Lent is the time for greater love, listen to Jesus' thirst' ...
'Repent and believe,' Jesus tells us. 'What are we to repent?'
Our indifference, our hardness of heart. What are we to
believe? Jesus thirsts even now, in your heart and in the poor —
He knows your weakness. He wants only your love, wants only
the chance to love you.'
ST TERESA OF KOLKATA

'You have taught us to overcome our sins by prayer,
fasting and works of mercy. When we are discouraged by
our weakness, give us confidence in your love.'
OPENING PRAYER

READ

Many Samaritans from that city believed in him because of
the woman's testimony, 'He told me everything I have ever
done.' So when the Samaritans came to him, they asked him
to stay with them; and he stayed there for two days. And many
more believed because of his word. They said to the woman,
'It is no longer because of what you said that we believe, for
we have heard for ourselves, and we know that this is truly
the Saviour of the world.' (Jn 4:39-42)

REFLECT

Have you ever had an unexpected conversation that prompted
you to think about something in a different manner? The
Samaritan woman became an unlikely person effecting a
change in her wider community. The Samaritans were not

Jewish. They were different. The fact that the Samaritan woman was able to have a life-changing encounter with Jesus is part of the story. She recognised Jesus offered something different. Obviously, something dramatic happened because we are told her community all began to seek out Jesus too. They all began to have individual encounters with Jesus and came to believe. Life-changing moments can take place in unexpected places.

Previous generations recalled stories of 'going to the well' to carry water back to their houses. It is only in recent generations that we have had water piped into our homes thanks to modern sanitation. Having access to clean water is one of our basic requirements. Going to the well was a social occasion. Conversation took place while people toiled and carried the water. Today, we have water coolers in our places of work.

Often, we hear of countries where the water supply gets contaminated due to flooding, pollution or a catastrophic weather event. Real people, often poor, experience great hardship. It is up to others to offer their support in such a crisis. Aid agencies play a vital role in reaching into these communities to help, assist and rebuild.

The next time we pour a glass of water, take a moment to remember those who do not have access to this life-saving resource. Do not take it for granted. The next time someone asks you for some 'water' remember the woman at the well who wasn't judged.

RESPOND

- In your life, where do you meet people? Where is your 'well'?

- Where do you source your water? Are you conscious of how you use/waste water?

- Have you considered limiting your 'plastic bottle' water usage and using sustainable water carriers?

MONDAY

'My soul is waiting for the Lord, I count on his word, because with the Lord there is mercy and fullness of redemption.'
'I believe my life has a purpose; I believe there is something after this; I believe that there is a big picture and I believe there is a God who is supporting me through this.'

FR TONY COOTE

🌙 READ

Today, slowly read the following passage from scripture and ponder each line carefully

And he said, 'Truly I tell you, no prophet is accepted in the prophet's hometown. But the truth is, there were many widows in Israel in the time of Elijah, when the heaven was shut up for three years and six months, and there was a severe famine over all the land; yet Elijah was sent to none of them except to a widow at Zarephath in Sidon. There were also many lepers in Israel in the time of the prophet Elisha, and none of them was cleansed except Naaman the Syrian.' When they heard this, all in the synagogue were filled with rage. They got up, drove him out of the town, and led him to the brow of the hill on which their town was built, so that they might hurl him off the cliff. But he passed through the midst of them and went on his way. (Lk 4:24-30)

🌙 REFLECT

The desire for healing is part of our human condition. When we become ill, we go to the doctor. Some turn to God. Often the question is 'why me?' Suffering and sickness are connected. In the Bible we read about those who were sick, especially the lepers who were kept on the edges of the community and lived apart. In the Old Testament, only Naaman was cured of leprosy. Jesus was well known for his healing and curing of the sick. In Nazara, we are told that Jesus was almost killed by those who were worshipping in the synagogue, especially when he mentioned the curing of Naaman. One of the great traditions of our faith are the various ceremonies that take place with people praying for healing. A 'healing mass' is usually made up of the faithful who have various forms of visible and invisible illnesses. There is also the tradition of people trying to 'touch' or be blessed by relics of saints and holy people. The compassion of those who try to assist the sick in hallowed sites such as Lourdes or Knock is a reminder that we who are blessed with good health have a lot to learn from those who are sick and turn to God for comfort. During Lent, as we yearn to be closer to God, consider being closer to those carrying various 'crosses'.

RESPOND

• If you suffer from an illness or sickness, pray to God today for strength and for those who help you.

• If you are healthy, reflect on those you know who are dealing with health issues, physical or mental, or ongoing complications. Reach out to them with acts of kindness, without condition.

TUESDAY

'I arise today, through God's strength to pilot me, God's might to uphold me, God's wisdom to guide me, God's eye to look before me, God's ear to hear me, God's word to speak for me, God's hand to guard me, God's way to lie before me, God's shield to protect me, God's host to save me.'

ST PATRICK'S BREASTPLATE

'The sinner of today is the saint of tomorrow. What is a saint, after all, other than a forgiven sinner.'

MEISTER ECKHART

✒ READ

Today, slowly read the following passage from scripture and ponder each line carefully

Make me to know your ways, O Lord; teach me your paths.

Lead me in your truth, and teach me, for you are the God of my salvation; for you I wait all day long.

Be mindful of your mercy, O Lord, and of your steadfast love, for they have been from of old.

Do not remember the sins of my youth or my transgressions; according to your steadfast love remember me, for your goodness' sake, O Lord!

Good and upright is the Lord; therefore, he instructs sinners in the way.

He leads the humble in what is right and teaches the humble his way. (Ps 25:4-9)

✒ REFLECT

Have you ever asked for forgiveness? Sometimes it is not easy. It is difficult. Have you ever received forgiveness? There is something humbling in asking for forgiveness. Catholics are invited to receive the Sacrament of Reconciliation regularly. There is nothing more powerful than watching, from afar, someone going to confession and seeing the priest pray and offer forgiveness. There is a noticeable change in the penitent. You can almost see their burdens lifted. Their slate has been wiped clean and a fresh start beckons. God's mercy is always on offer. We are not meant to hold on to our sins or whatever is keeping us from a full relationship with God. It is healthy to be in right relations with God. This also extends to those to whom we need to offer an apology or seek forgiveness. Jesus reminds us to offer forgiveness 'from the heart'. Forgiveness begins when we realise in our heart that God's mercy is unending. Our lenten path is one that will bring us to Calvary; even in his dying breath the thief asked for forgiveness. It is never too late.

RESPOND

• Being a Christian involves being able to forgive. Today, reflect on how forgiving you are as person. Do you need to adjust anything in your life to make yourself more forgiving?

• Catholics are invited to avail of the Sacrament of Reconciliation. Consider arranging to go to confession during Lent. If you are a Christian, consider going to your local faith leader and asking for a prayer for forgiveness. Mercy has no boundaries.

WEDNESDAY

'Please, thank you and sorry, are words that open up the road to a good family life.'
POPE FRANCIS

'Our highest human goal is to encounter God. We are born from love, kept alive by love, and fullness of life comes when we recognise this love and freely embrace it. But many people today, sadly, cannot glimpse or perceive this intimate calling.'
POPE FRANCIS

READ

Today, slowly read the following passage from scripture and ponder each line carefully

See, just as the Lord my God has charged me, I now teach you statutes and ordinances for you to observe in the land that you are about to enter and occupy. You must observe them diligently, for this will show your wisdom and discernment to the peoples, who, when they hear all these statutes, will say, 'Surely this great nation is a wise and discerning people!' For what other great nation has a god so near to it as the Lord our God is whenever we call to him? And what other great nation has statutes and ordinances as just as this entire law that I am setting before you today?

But take care and watch yourselves closely, so as neither to forget the things that your eyes have seen nor to let them slip from your mind all the days of your life; make them known to your children and your children's children. (Deut 4:5-9)

REFLECT

Great care and attention are invested in the process of trying to pass on the key tenets of our faith. With so many competing demands on their resources, however, it can often be difficult for parents and educators to devote enough time to this fundamental activity. A key element of our faith is receiving what has been passed on from generation to generation. In the past it may have seemed to be a less onerous task: culture and convention assisted the teaching of faith. During Lent there will be many adults participating in the Rite of Christian Initiation. They will spend a great amount of time learning about faith and its ritual, tradition and law. In a sense during Lent every one of us should reflect on our faith, beginning with our Baptism. While it might seem people know less about their faith today and practise it less frequently, Jesus is reminding us not to popularise our faith, but express and live it in a more meaningful and challenging way. Anyone who follows Jesus has the promise of having the 'light of life'. Passing on our faith is not easy, but is it the correct response to God. This Lent, maybe it is time for us to re-establish our understanding of the faith we seek to pass on.

RESPOND

• Take a moment to reflect on the commandments.
• What memories do you have of traditions of faith in your family?
• What traditions would you like to pass on to the next generation?

THURSDAY

'The greatest figures of prophecy and sanctity step forth out
of the darkness night ... the decisive moments of history are
determined by souls whom no history book ever mentions.'

ST EDITH STEIN

'Christ has no body now but yours, no hand,
no feet on earth but yours.'

ST TERESA OF AVILA

READ

Today, slowly read the following passage from scripture and ponder each line carefully
Now the birth of Jesus the Messiah took place in this way.
When his mother Mary had been engaged to Joseph, but
before they lived together, she was found to be with child
from the Holy Spirit. Her husband Joseph, being a righteous
man and unwilling to expose her to public disgrace, planned
to dismiss her quietly. But just when he had resolved to do
this, an angel of the Lord appeared to him in a dream and
said, 'Joseph, son of David, do not be afraid to take Mary as
your wife, for the child conceived in her is from the Holy
Spirit. She will bear a son, and you are to name him Jesus, for
he will save his people from their sins.' All this took place to
fulfil what had been spoken by the Lord through the prophet.
(Mt 1:18-22)

REFLECT

Saint Joseph is one of the most understated people in the New
Testament. He was a quiet man about whom we know very
little. What we do know is that he did have a relationship with

61

God; he responded to God's call to take care of Mary. He was chosen by God to lead his family through rough times. He had a deep sense of God's calling. Joseph said 'yes' to God in silent ways. First he supported the pregnant Mary, then Mary the new mother and soon he was the father helping Mary find Jesus when he seemed to be lost. The humble carpenter's son was influenced by the carpenter and lived 'under their authority'. Even though Jesus was the Son of God it can be assumed that Mary and Joseph had a major influence during Jesus' formative years. No matter how influential or famous a son or daughter becomes in life, every person has a mother or father. Joseph is sometimes identified as the worker. Today we remember all those parents who work tirelessly to support their children. Children often don't notice the sacrifice that parents make for them. We are all someone's son or daughter, so today we remember all those who work on behalf of others, to create a better world and create opportunities for others to flourish.

RESPOND

• God worked; God rested. How do you create balance in your life between what you do and who you are?

• There are many who either have no job or can't work for one reason or another. Take time to pray for those who are not blessed by the gift of meaningful employment in your community.

FRIDAY

*'So, I said to the Lord, "You promised me Lord, that if I
followed you, you would walk with me always. But I have
noticed that during the most trying periods of my life there
have only been one set of footprints in the sand.
Why when I needed you most, have you not been there
for me?" The Lord replied, "The times when you have seen
only one set of footprints, my child, is when I carried you." '*

MARY STEVENSON

*'I know God will not give me anything I can't handle.
I just wish that he didn't trust me so much" '*

ST TERESA OF KOLKATA

READ

Today, slowly read the following passage from scripture and ponder each line carefully

One of the scribes came near and heard them disputing with
one another, and seeing that he answered them well, he asked
him, 'Which commandment is the first of all?' Jesus answered,
'The first is, "Hear, O Israel: the Lord our God, the Lord is
one; you shall love the Lord your God with all your heart, and
with all your soul, and with all your mind, and with all your
strength." The second is this, "You shall love your neighbour
as yourself." There is no other commandment greater than
these.' Then the scribe said to him, 'You are right, Teacher;
you have truly said that "he is one, and besides him there is
no other"; and "to love him with all the heart, and with all
the understanding, and with all the strength", and "to love
one's neighbour as oneself", – this is much more important

than all whole burnt-offerings and sacrifices.' When Jesus saw that he answered wisely, he said to him, 'You are not far from the kingdom of God.' After that no one dared to ask him any question. (Mk 12:28-34)

REFLECT

We all mess up every now and again. Everyone can make a mistake. Not everyone is a winner. As Christians, it is important to know that we strive towards perfection and holiness. Even Jesus stumbled as he carried his cross. He met people on his way who offered him assistance. During his ministry Jesus helped people in unexpected ways. As we journey towards the middle of Lent it is good to look back to see how we are carried along by others, by God, during difficult moments. Being able to get up and start again is important. Being able to help others start again is also important. Being able to accompany others on their journey towards personal recovery or discovery can help. Just being present for others is important.

RESPOND

• Show your gratitude to someone who helped you at some point in your life. Offer them a prayer today.

• Whenever you 'failed' at something, who helped you back up? Have you in turn helped someone who needed help?

• Loving God and expressing that can be challenging. How do you express God's love for you and for others?

SATURDAY

'Dear Jesus, help me to spread
Your fragrance everywhere I go.
Flood my soul with your spirit and your life.
Penetrate and possess my whole being so utterly,
That all my life may be only
A radiance of yours.'

ST JOHN HENRY NEWMAN

⟩ READ

Today, slowly read the following passage from scripture and ponder each line carefully

Come, let us return to the Lord; for it is he who has torn, and he will heal us; he has struck down, and he will bind us up.

After two days he will revive us; on the third day he will raise us up, that we may live before him.

Let us know, let us press on to know the Lord; his appearing is as sure as the dawn; he will come to us like the showers, like the spring rains that water the earth.

What shall I do with you, O Ephraim? What shall I do with you, O Judah?

Your love is like a morning cloud, like the dew that goes away early.

Therefore I have hewn them by the prophets, I have killed them by the words of my mouth, and my judgement goes forth as the light.

For I desire steadfast love and not sacrifice, the knowledge of God rather than burnt-offerings. (Hos 6:1-6)

REFLECT

We are all invited to live and express our faith. Another word for this is 'witness'. How we do this has implications for those who are near us. Jesus had harsh words for those who were keen to draw attention to themselves in the act of prayer. In highlighting their faith in an ostentatious manner, they were simply trying to impress those around them. We have all seen people express their faith in such ways. Jesus reminds us that the pillars and leaders of faith can sometimes distract us from what is important in expressing faith. We have all seen 'pharisees' go over the top in their expression or devotion of faith. That might even be one of us at times. We have seen the pharisees fall from grace as their parallel lives were exposed and their hypocrisy revealed. Jesus draws our attention to the Tax Collector. His plea for God's mercy was honest. His relationship with God was restored. This Lent, begin with yourself, orientate your life towards God and have the humility to raise your eyes upwards, rather than towards those who are watching you.

RESPOND

• Do you spend time telling others how to live their faith? Or do you just get on with living your own faith?
• Can you be really honest with God and ask for God's mercy?
• As we conclude this third week of Lent, may our lenten observance of the suffering, death and Resurrection of Christ bring us to the full joy of Easter.

FOURTH WEEK OF LENT

SUNDAY
'The Lord rubbed my eyes: I went away and washed;
then I could see, and I believed in God.'
COMMUNION ANTIPHON

'Amazing grace. How sweet the sound that saved
a wretch like me. I once was lost, but now I'm found,
was blind, but now I see.'
AMAZING GRACE

READ
Today, slowly read the following passage from scripture and ponder each line carefully
The Lord is my shepherd; I shall not want. He makes me lie down in green pastures; he leads me beside still waters; he restores my soul. He leads me in right paths for his name's sake. Even though I walk through the darkest valley, I fear no evil; for you are with me; your rod and your staff they comfort me. (Ps 23:1-4)

REFLECT
In the Gospels we often read about Jesus reaching out to those on the margins and highlighting their plight. Jesus often used the weak and vulnerable to make a point and to challenge those in positions of power. This led to conflict of opinion. Sometimes those who are on the margins of a community have very poor self-esteem. Jesus had a message for everyone. He was able to make the blind man see. He was also able to 'annoy' the establishment and challenge the elite to do more for others. Sometimes we need help. When people are feeling down, depressed, or need our love and support,

it is important for each of us to respond in kind. Have you ever noticed the homeless person being offered food by a stranger? Sometimes no words are exchanged. We can all notice those on the edge of our community and respond accordingly. Pope Francis was told by a brother cardinal to 'never forget the poor'. Jesus is the shepherd leading us on the right path. As followers of Jesus this Lent our almsgiving can also take the form of practical service. We can all respond to the needy in our community. All it takes is for one person to respond. Acts of kindness are important. It is important that we do not remain blind to those around us who need assistance. The gaze of Jesus was powerful. We all need to see, so that we can truly believe.

RESPOND

• Find out what local charities are in your area and see if you can volunteer.

• Think of the people and groups on the margins of your community. How can you show your support to them?

MONDAY
'Lord I believe, help my unbelief.'
MARK 9:14

'The wonderous theme of the Bible that frightens so many
people is that the only visible sign of God in the world is the
cross. Christ is not carried away from earth to heaven in glory,
but he must go to the cross. And precisely there, where the cross
stands, the Resurrection is near; even there, where everyone
begins to doubt God, where everyone despairs of God's power,
there God is whole, there Christ is active and near. Where the
power of darkness does violence to the light of God, there God
triumphs and judges the darkness.'
DIETRICH BONHOEFFER

READ
Today, slowly read the following passage from scripture and ponder each line carefully
Then Jesus said to him, 'Unless you see signs and wonders
you will not believe.' The official said to him, 'Sir, come down
before my little boy dies.' Jesus said to him, 'Go; your son
will live.' The man believed the word that Jesus spoke to him
and started on his way. As he was going down, his slaves met
him and told him that his child was alive. So he asked them
the hour when he began to recover, and they said to him,
'Yesterday at one in the afternoon the fever left him.' The
father realised that this was the hour when Jesus had said to
him, 'Your son will live.' So he himself believed, along with
his whole household. Now this was the second sign that Jesus
did after coming from Judea to Galilee. (Jn 4:48-54)

REFLECT

Many people speak fondly of Jesus. Popular opinion would indicate that many follow Jesus. Some like him and what he did, but are not followers. Some people say they are spiritual but not religious. Putting your trust in Jesus also entails putting into action some of his words and deeds. In the New Testament there are stories of people who are not followers of Jesus, but who have an admiration for Jesus and still turn to him in times of need. Lent can be a time when people might reconsider the person of Jesus and his legacy. Pope Francis said, 'I invite all ... to a personal relationship with Jesus.' Being open to the Good News allows the possibility of Jesus having an ongoing presence in your life. Being open to people who have a very 'loose' faith or understanding of Jesus is also important. How often have believers been asked to pray for someone because those asking don't consider themselves religious? Being a mediary in such circumstances is a privilege. The joy of the court official came as a result of noticing what Jesus was doing and asking. It was the beginning of his faith journey. He was on 'his way'. Lent is a time for people to begin to invite Jesus to help them. This is their 'way' towards an ongoing encounter with Jesus.

RESPOND

• If you know of people who do not have a relationship with Jesus, be ready to witness to Jesus and your personal relationship. Don't force people to believe but invite them to follow.

• If you were to ask Jesus for help, what is the one request you would ask him?

TUESDAY

*'Come to the waters, all who thirst; though you have
no money, come and drink with joy.'*
ENTRANCE ANTIPHON

*'Within our darkest night, you kindle the fire
that never dies away, that never dies away.'*
TAIZÉ

READ

Today, slowly read the following passage from scripture and ponder each line carefully
One man was there who had been ill for thirty-eight years.
When Jesus saw him lying there and knew that he had been
there a long time, he said to him, 'Do you want to be made
well?' The sick man answered him, 'Sir, I have no one to put
me into the pool when the water is stirred up; and while I
am making my way, someone else steps down ahead of me.'
Jesus said to him, 'Stand up, take your mat and walk.' At once
the man was made well, and he took up his mat and began
to walk.

Now that day was a sabbath. So, the Jews said to the man
who had been cured, 'It is the sabbath; it is not lawful for
you to carry your mat.' But he answered them, 'The man who
made me well said to me, "Take up your mat and walk."' They
asked him, 'Who is the man who said to you, "Take it up and
walk"?' Now the man who had been healed did not know
who it was, for Jesus had disappeared in the crowd that was
there. Later Jesus found him in the temple and said to him,
'See, you have been made well! Do not sin anymore, so that
nothing worse happens to you.' The man went away and told

the Jews that it was Jesus who had made him well. Therefore, the Jews started persecuting Jesus, because he was doing such things on the sabbath. (Jn 5:5-16)

REFLECT

Some people find it difficult to ask for help; they know they need assistance but are reluctant to ask. Sometimes people become resigned to remaining in a rut – be it emotional or otherwise – because they can't see a way out. This sense of inertia can take many forms. Those experiencing addiction of various kinds may, for instance, struggle to seek help, out of a misguided sense of embarrassment. In John's Gospel, we are told that Jesus 'saw' the sick man and asked him if he wished to be well. The gaze of Jesus can be penetrating. Jesus' intervention was all that it took for the man to change course. The man we are told responded to Jesus' invitation to get up. It took him a while to recognise that is was Jesus who helped him. All around us, there are many in need of help. Never underestimate the power of asking someone that very simple question: 'Can I help?' Your intervention may be just enough to point them in a new direction.

RESPOND

• There are many people who need different kinds of help. Are you someone who makes time to volunteer in your community or assist those in your life who need you?
• Did someone reach out to you in a time of difficulty? Today, say a prayer for that person.

WEDNESDAY

'Our "Yes" to God — this transformation, this transfiguration of persons and of the world — is not just a dream, a mere fantasy. It is the frequent experience of any Christian who one day understands that, if God is Love, and that he or she is the object of this love, it is impossible not to abandon self trustingly to him'.

CHIARA LUBICH

'Angel of God, my guardian dear, to whom God's love commits me here, ever this day, be at my side to light and guard, to rule and guide.'

TRADITIONAL PRAYER

➥ READ

Today, slowly read the following passage from scripture and ponder each line carefully
In the sixth month the angel Gabriel was sent by God to a town in Galilee called Nazareth, to a virgin engaged to a man whose name was Joseph, of the house of David. The virgin's name was Mary. And he came to her and said, 'Greetings, favoured one! The Lord is with you.' But she was much perplexed by his words and pondered what sort of greeting this might be. The angel said to her, 'Do not be afraid, Mary, for you have found favour with God. And now, you will conceive in your womb and bear a son, and you will name him Jesus. He will be great and will be called the Son of the Most High, and the Lord God will give to him the throne of his ancestor David. He will reign over the house of Jacob for ever, and of his kingdom there will be no end.' Mary said to the angel, 'How can this be, since I am a virgin?' The

angel said to her, 'The Holy Spirit will come upon you, and the power of the Most High will overshadow you; therefore the child to be born will be holy; he will be called Son of God. And now, your relative Elizabeth in her old age has also conceived a son; and this is the sixth month for her who was said to be barren. For nothing will be impossible with God.' Then Mary said, 'Here am I, the servant of the Lord; let it be with me according to your word.' Then the angel departed from her. (Lk 1:26-38)

REFLECT

Are you more inclined to say 'yes' or 'no' to a request? Sometimes our responses are both immediate and instinctive – we do not have to think very hard about how we will reply. Mary, we are told, was 'disturbed' by what the angel had told her. Being afraid is natural when something unexpected happens. Nobody expects God to send an emissary to them with such astounding news! Mary did not anticipate a message being sent by God. However, as she quickly reflected on this new invitation, new challenge, she stepped into the unknown. Her gut feeling was her God feeling. Mary said 'yes' to God. Saying 'yes' to God is important because we know that God will only ask us to do something that we are capable of doing. God's revelation to Mary was indeed a new stage in her relationship with God. God is constantly revealing himself to us, in words, deeds, messages and signs. Look around you today to see what God is calling you to be. Do you dare to say 'yes'?

RESPOND

• On this day take time to reflect on any occasion you felt inclined to say yes to something or someone.

• Many people try to discern what they would like to do in life. It is important to know what path you are on – do not be afraid to ask for help in making decisions that could change how you live the rest of your life.

THURSDAY

'Lead, kindly light, amid the encircling gloom,
lead thou me on! The night is dark, and I am far from home,
lead thou me on! Keep thou my feet, I do not ask to see the
distant scene; one step enough for me.'

ST JOHN HENRY NEWMAN

'O Creator of the universe, source of light and wisdom, thou
mighty beginning of all things, enlighten the dullness of my
perception with the light of thy clarity and take from me
the darkness of sin and ignorance. Give me intelligence to
understand, good memory to retain, the capacity to discern
rightly and thoroughly delicacy and exactitude in explanation,
fullness and grace of expression. Teach the beginning, guide the
unfolding, help in the completion ...'

ST THOMAS AQUINAS

✎ READ

Today, slowly read the following passage from scripture and ponder each line carefully

But Moses implored the Lord his God, and said, 'O Lord,
why does your wrath burn hot against your people, whom
you brought out of the land of Egypt with great power and
with a mighty hand? Why should the Egyptians say, "It was
with evil intent that he brought them out to kill them in the
mountains, and to consume them from the face of the earth"?
Turn from your fierce wrath; change your mind and do not
bring disaster on your people. Remember Abraham, Isaac,
and Israel, your servants, how you swore to them by your
own self, saying to them, "I will multiply your descendants

like the stars of heaven, and all this land that I have promised I will give to your descendants, and they shall inherit it for ever."' And the Lord changed his mind about the disaster that he planned to bring on his people. (Ex 32:11-14)

REFLECT

In Europe, many have abandoned the practice of Christianity. Secularism has taken hold in many countries. Traditional ways of believing and belonging have been impacted by successive generations choosing to live lives free of the teachings of Jesus. There are many complex reasons for this. Emigration and being uprooted can lead to a sense of being disconnected. Many became disillusioned with the Church as a result of how the hierarchy dealt with sexual abuse scandals. Families also lost the ability to pass on faith. Many Church leaders failed to respond and pastorally lead in a time of change. As God said to Moses, 'They were quick to leave the way I marked out for them.' Rituals and practices of religion have been replaced by secular substitutes. History has a knack of repeating itself. Just when neighbours, family and friends abandon their beliefs it challenges each of us in how we continue to be faithful. Lent helps each of us to deal with forms of belief and unbelief. God's promise and invitation to walk in his path is not a populist one. You do not follow God because you want the approval of your friends. It is the same for those who abandon their faith in order to be popular among their peers. God wants authentic followers, not snowflakes that can melt. Being a disciple is not easy. Being a disciple is really the road less travelled.

RESPOND

- Do you have moments of belief and unbelief? What is this like? What do you do to counteract feelings of unbelief?
- How do you react when someone or something challenges your faith in God? What do you do?

FRIDAY

'For all the more reason, then, should evil speech be curbed so that punishment for sin may be avoided. Indeed, so important is silence that permission to speak should seldom be granted even to mature disciples, no matter how good or holy or constructive their talk ... Speaking and teaching are the master's task; the disciple is to be silent and listen.'

RULE OF ST BENEDICT

'Settle yourself in solitude and you will come upon him in yourself ... Don't imagine that we need wings to go in search of him. We have only to find a place where we can be alone and look upon him present within us.'

ST TERESA OF AVILA

READ

Today, slowly read the following passage from scripture and ponder each line carefully
Thus they reasoned, but they were led astray, for their wickedness blinded them, and they did not know the secret purposes of God, nor hoped for the wages of holiness, nor discerned the prize for blameless souls. (Wis 2:20-22)

REFLECT

As Lent progresses you might at times wonder why you are taking part in the onerous exercises and duties that are the cornerstone of the season. Thoughts of 'why bother?' understandably cross your mind. It is a challenge to recommit to your decision at the beginning of Lent. We are invited to persevere in times of adversity and trust in the Lord. Being

faithful to your personal decisions to enter more meaningfully in Lent is between you and God. It is personal. It is okay to privatise your personal spiritual journey. Take solace that at certain times, as Jesus drew near Jerusalem, he 'went quietly, without drawing attention to himself'. One of the challenges is to know when to be very bold in proclaiming and living your message of faith. Sometimes it is fine to pray in private and live your faith in a private way, so long as you know that you will still have to go to your Jerusalem. The shadow of Holy Week and the draw of Jerusalem are getting stronger. Sometimes doing less in public has a greater impact than all the public appearances we might be tempted to put in.

RESPOND

• Have you ever experienced personal or 'private' moments of faith, where you connect to the Lord in order to help you and your prayer life? Maybe today, try to take a moment to step outside your normal routine without drawing attention to yourself and reconnect with the Lord.

• Do you spend more time wondering if you are seen at key religious events or are you someone who is happy to attend without being seen?

• Jesus gradually becomes unpopular for his views and actions. Are you prepared to follow this path?

SATURDAY

*'Guide us in your gentle mercy, for left to ourselves
we cannot do your will.'*
OPENING PRAYER

**'Lent, thus, is a call to celebrate our redemption in that difficult
combination of cross and victory. Our people are well prepared
to do so these days; all our environment proclaims the cross.
But those who have Christian faith and hope know that behind
this Calvary of El Salvador lies our Easter, our Resurrection.
This is the Christian people's hope.'**
ÓSCAR ROMERO

READ

Today, slowly read the following passage from scripture and ponder each line carefully
It was the Lord who made it known to me, and I knew; then
you showed me their evil deeds. But I was like a gentle lamb
led to the slaughter. And I did not know it was against me that
they devised schemes, saying, 'Let us destroy the tree with its
fruit, let us cut him off from the land of the living, so that
his name will no longer be remembered!' But you, O Lord
of hosts, who judge righteously, who try the heart and the
mind, let me see your retribution upon them, for to you I
have committed my cause. (Jer 11:18-20)

REFLECT

We live in a world where very little of what happens remains
secret. Social media, gossip pages and the allure of irrelevant
news can distract us from keeping our focus on what truly
matters. It can be difficult to be a follower of Jesus today. You

can be ridiculed for espousing a faith that your 'enlightened' peers have abandoned. In families today it can be harder to continue to be a committed believer because some family members no longer practise their faith. The sins of Church leaders have had an immeasurable impact on people in abandoning their faith. Jesus attracted many observers. Some went on to be amazing followers, disciples, saints and scholars. Others chose paths that corrupted and diminished those who were attempting to follow Jesus. History is filled with examples of people who have selflessly given their lives because they refused to renounce their faith. The early Church was established on the blood of the first Martyrs. In Ireland we had the Irish Martyrs during penal times. In the twentieth century, which saw untold carnage during two World Wars, people such as Maximilian Kolbe gave their lives to save others. Many in our world today are judgemental of those who follow in Christ's footsteps and endeavour to live out the Gospel values. We must never lose focus simply because we are ridiculed or ignored. This is not easy. No one said it was.

RESPOND

• Reflect on the amount of time you spend thinking about other people and what they get up to. This could be in your local community or through social media. Are you a follower of the gossip pages or are your someone who tries to see the good in others? Maybe today, assess how prudent you are in judging others around you.

• Maybe you have misjudged others at times. How did you make amends?

FIFTH WEEK OF LENT

SUNDAY

'... help us to be like Christ your Son, who loved the world and died for our salvation.'

ENTRANCE ANTIPHON

'Our Lord came down to earth out of compassion for the human race. He suffered our sufferings on the cross, before taking our flesh. Indeed, if he had not suffered, he would not have come down to share our sufferings.'

ORIGEN OF ALEXANDRIA

READ

Today, slowly read the following passage from scripture and ponder each line carefully

When Jesus arrived, he found that Lazarus had already been in the tomb for four days. Now Bethany was near Jerusalem, some two miles away, and many of the Jews had come to Martha and Mary to console them about their brother. When Martha heard that Jesus was coming, she went and met him, while Mary stayed at home. Martha said to Jesus, 'Lord, if you had been here, my brother would not have died. But even now I know that God will give you whatever you ask of him.' Jesus said to her, 'Your brother will rise again.' Martha said to him, 'I know that he will rise again in the resurrection on the last day.' Jesus said to her, 'I am the resurrection and the life. Those who believe in me, even though they die, will live, and everyone who lives and believes in me will never die. Do you believe this?' She said to him, 'Yes, Lord, I believe that you are the Messiah, the Son of God, the one coming into the world.' (Jn 11:17-24)

REFLECT

Don't give up. As we journey into the penultimate week of Lent there might be a tendency to let things slide. We might be tempted to relax in our commitment. Long distance athletes speak about 'hitting a wall', a reference to the moment in a race or an event where they feel they want to stop or have nothing left to give. Somehow, they dig deep and find the reserves of energy they need to continue. We need to know that, as we journey toward Holy Week and dig deeper into our faith, somewhere in that despair or unknowing we can find the grace to continue. Belief is a powerful concept. It can propel us into doing amazing things for other people. Belief is knowing who to ask for help when the possible can seem impossible. For Mary and Martha, Jesus made the impossible possible in raising Lazarus. They turned to Jesus and asked for help when it seemed there was nowhere else to turn. Knowing when to dig deep in order to finish the race is crucial as we strive to observe our lenten observances. God knows we are doing our best, even if at times we have fallen short in our lenten promises. God loves us unconditionally. We are called to love God also. We are reminded that anything that distracts us from experiencing or expressing that love is not pleasing to God. During this week of Lent, try to please God by digging deeper. There is a finish line and even if you think you cannot reach it, God is with you every step of the way. God's mercy is deep. It is only when we go deeper into our relationship with God that we experience the grace and strength to further in our relationship with him.

RESPOND

• Nothing is impossible to God. Has something 'died' in your life, something that Jesus could restore?

• When did you last use the words: 'Yes Lord, I believe.' Today try to repeat those words and believe.

MONDAY

'Father, I put myself into your hands; Father, I abandon myself
to you: I entrust myself to you. Father, do with me as it
please you. Whatever you do with me, I will thank you for it.
Giving thanks for anything I am ready for anything;
I give thanks for anything.'
BLESSED CHARLES DE FOUCAULD

'Bear the cross and do not make the cross bear you.'
ST PHILIP NERI

READ

Today, slowly read the following passage from scripture and ponder each line carefully
The scribes and the Pharisees brought a woman who had
been caught in adultery; and making her stand before all of
them, they said to him, 'Teacher, this woman was caught in
the very act of committing adultery. Now in the law Moses
commanded us to stone such women. Now what do you
say?' They said this to test him, so that they might have some
charge to bring against him. Jesus bent down and wrote with
his finger on the ground. When they kept on questioning
him, he straightened up and said to them, 'Let anyone among
you who is without sin be the first to throw a stone at her.'
And once again he bent down and wrote on the ground.
When they heard it, they went away, one by one, beginning
with the elders; and Jesus was left alone with the woman
standing before him. Jesus straightened up and said to her,
'Woman, where are they? Has no one condemned you?' She
said, 'No one, sir.' And Jesus said, 'Neither do I condemn you.
Go your way, and from now on do not sin again.' (Jn 8:3-11)

REFLECT

We have all encountered people who like to gossip. Gossip can really destroy and harm people. Those who conspire to undermine, hurt or damage an individual's or a community's reputation are capable of great harm. These people often hide behind avatars on social media and are cowardly in their behaviour. At other times they use their status in society or the role they have in a community to inflict hurt on others. The cunningness of these people is far reaching. They try to hide in plain sight and can seem untouchable. When those people who enjoy such activities are caught out, however, the fall from grace is swift. Joachim and Susanna were wronged by gossip and inuendo. A miscarriage of justice almost occurred. Those who accused Susanna of adultery were found out and God's judgement was swift. Jesus demonstrated how those who have sinned should refrain from judging others. Jesus offered mercy to the sinner to 'go your way, and from now on do not sin again'. The challenge for each of us is to distance ourselves from the gossipers and those who try to destroy people's character. Bullies don't like being challenged. During these last days of Lent, as the shadow of the cross is cast upon the land, let us use our words to build people up, not to destroy them.

RESPOND

• Are you ever guilty of taking pleasure in the suffering of another? How can I overcome this tendency and reach out to those who have wronged me?

• Take time this week to compliment or thank someone in your life whom you may have overlooked or misjudged.

TUESDAY
'Put your hope in the Lord. Take courage and be strong.'
OPENING ANTIPHON

'When you think about it, you should not let yourself be
pressurised by life ... If no one can keep death away from you
then no one has ultimate power. All power is pretension.
No one avoids death. Therefore, the world should never
persuade you of its power over your, since it has no power
whatever to keep death away from you ... If you learn not to
be afraid of your death, then you realise you do not need to
fear anything else either.'
JOHN O'DONOHUE

READ
Today, slowly read the following passage from the scripture and ponder each line carefully
They set out by the way to the Red Sea, to go around the land
of Edom; but the people became impatient on the way. The
people spoke against God and against Moses, 'Why have you
brought us up out of Egypt to die in the wilderness? For there
is no food and no water, and we detest this miserable food.'

Then the Lord sent poisonous serpents among the people,
and they bit the people, so that many Israelites died. The
people came to Moses and said, 'We have sinned by speaking
against the Lord and against you; pray to the Lord to take
away the serpents from us.' So Moses prayed for the people.
And the Lord said to Moses, 'Make a poisonous serpent, and
set it on a pole; and everyone who is bitten shall look at it and
live.' So Moses made a serpent of bronze, and put it upon a

pole; and whenever a serpent bit someone, that person would look at the serpent of bronze and live. (Num 21:4-9)

REFLECT

Those who continue to practise their faith, even when times are tough, can sometimes lose patience. They attend church each week, say their prayers and do their best to be a good person; however, there may come a moment when they question their faith, especially at a time when so many have left the Church because they've found it wanting. We have all observed how, in recent years, the Church congregation has become greyer and older. Contrast this with popular culture where everything is youthful and vibrant. Somewhere on this journey of faith, 'people lost patience' and just stopped or abandoned their faith. We are not the first generation of people to deny God. It can be disheartening to notice more empty pews than full ones. Jesus was aware that popularity is transient. He did say, 'I am going away; you will look for me.' People have abandoned the Church but are still searching for happiness in various ways. Jesus knew that people would have to dig deeper in order to continue to be with him. Some people have never really encountered Jesus. Many who attend Church can also relate to this. It is only when we personally reflect on the magnitude of what Jesus did for each of us through his life, death and Resurrection that we really come to believe in him. It is only then that we can establish a personal relationship with him. However, it is not enough just to believe, we must also belong. Jesus is the centre around which we gather to remember and renew our relationship with him.

RESPOND

• Are there times that you become impatient with your faith or even your faith community? How?

• In what ways can your faith attract those who have 'lost patience' with their own?

• Is there something you can do to help people come to a deeper understanding of who Jesus was?

• Is there anything you can do in your parish community to be more welcoming to those who wish to search, learn and encounter faith in a more meaningful way?

WEDNESDAY
'Hear the prayers of your repentant children who
call on you in love.'
OPENING PRAYER

'This is our God the servant king, He calls us now to follow
Him — to bring our lives as a daily offering of worship to the
servant king.'
THE SERVANT KING, HYMN

READ
Today, slowly read the following passage from scripture and ponder each line carefully
Then Jesus said to the Jews who had believed in him, 'If you continue in my word, you are truly my disciples; and you will know the truth, and the truth will make you free.' They answered him, 'We are descendants of Abraham and have never been slaves to anyone. What do you mean by saying, "You will be made free"?' Jesus answered them, 'Very truly, I tell you, everyone who commits sin is a slave to sin. The slave does not have a permanent place in the household; the son has a place there for ever. So if the Son makes you free, you will be free indeed. I know that you are descendants of Abraham; yet you look for an opportunity to kill me, because there is no place in you for my word. I declare what I have seen in the Father's presence; as for you, you should do what you have heard from the Father.' (Jn 8:31-35)

REFLECT

Ultimately Lent is about hope. Lent is a time that is set aside to reflect on your personal relationship with Jesus. It is a time to reflect on how much of an impact he has on how you live and orientate your life. Sometimes we dwell on our past mistakes so much that we forget to live in the present. The past can also give us clues as to who we are. Having a connection with your family going back generations can be helpful. The Jewish followers of Jesus often reflected on their connection to Abraham as his descendants. Sometimes our family history can impede our growth. Jesus offered to those who followed him a new freedom. This liberty comes from making 'his word your home'. Sometimes noticing the people who surround you, especially family members, creates a unique connection. Being connected to Jesus also means being connected to God. Jesus was sent by his father as an act of love. In these last days of Lent, maybe have a closer look at the person of Jesus and continue to dwell on what he did for each of us. It is easy to criticise him or take his words for granted. Reconnect with his words and mission. His mission is also our mission.

RESPOND

• Take some time out this day to give thanks for the family you are from. No family is perfect, but it is still our family.
• If there is a member of your family you are distant from, consider doing an act of kindness for that person, even merely lighting a candle for them.

THURSDAY

'We also have to look at the elderly, because the elderly are full of wisdom. Listen to what the elderly have to say.'
POPE FRANCIS

READ

Today, slowly read the following passage from scripture and ponder each line carefully

Then Abram fell on his face; and God said to him, 'As for me, this is my covenant with you: You shall be the ancestor of a multitude of nations. No longer shall your name be Abram, but your name shall be Abraham; for I have made you the ancestor of a multitude of nations. I will make you exceedingly fruitful; and I will make nations of you, and kings shall come from you. I will establish my covenant between me and you, and your offspring after you throughout their generations, for an everlasting covenant, to be God to you and to your offspring after you. And I will give to you, and to your offspring after you, the land where you are now an alien, all the land of Canaan, for a perpetual holding; and I will be their God.' (Gn 17:3-8)

REFLECT

One of the most influential groups in our society are grandparents. They are very underrated. Not every person has had the privilege to know their grandparents. Children who have the gift of being able to get to know them are privileged. Grandparents and older generations have much to teach and pass on. The lives of many young parents are challenging, but to have grandparents take some of the load off is an amazing gift. Children love to hear the stories about 'the old days'. Jesus was surrounded by people who often harked back to Abraham.

Jesus told the Jews that he knew Abraham. He also told them that before 'Abraham ever was, I Am.' It was a confusing time and emotions were running high. Jesus was able to connect with his ancestors in a way that at the time people did not understand. Grandparents can help this current generation make sense of their family and where each of us comes from. Our grandparents are like a mirror and reflect something about who we are and where we come from. Sometimes we might like what we see or at times we might not. As Christians following Jesus, we can look at him and notice the connection. Our faith was passed on to us. Our challenge is to accept it and pass it on to future generations. In order to do this, we need to get to know more about our Christian family and its origins.

RESPOND

• What memories and stories do you recall being told by some of the older members of your family? Have you spoken about these to younger generations?

• Make an effort to gather your family or attend the next family event. These moments are special.

• Have a conversation with some older people about what they remember when they were growing up? It is good to talk and to pass on these stories to younger generations.

FRIDAY

'O God, author of every mercy and of all goodness, who in fasting, prayer and almsgiving have shown us a remedy for sin, look graciously on this confession of our lowliness, that we, who are bowed down by our conscience, may always be lifted up by your mercy...'
THE COLLECT

'May the Lord support us all the day long till the shades lengthen and the evening comes, and the busy world is hushed, and the fever of life is over and our work is done. Then in his mercy, may he give us a safe lodging and a holy rest and peace at the last.'
ST JOHN HENRY NEWMAN

'Jesus carried our sins in his own body on the cross so that we could die to sin and live in holiness: by his wounds we have been healed.'
COMMUNION ANTIPHON

READ

Today, slowly read the following passage from scripture and ponder each line carefully
For I hear many whispering: 'Terror is all around! Denounce him! Let us denounce him!' All my close friends are watching for me to stumble. 'Perhaps he can be enticed, and we can prevail against him, and take our revenge on him.' But the Lord is with me like a dread warrior; therefore my persecutors will stumble, and they will not prevail.

They will be greatly shamed, for they will not succeed. Their eternal dishonour will never be forgotten. O Lord of hosts, you test the righteous, you see the heart and the mind; let me see your retribution upon them, for to you I have committed my cause.

Sing to the Lord; praise the Lord! For he has delivered the life of the needy from the hands of evildoers. (Jer 20:10-13)

REFLECT

There is little doubt that as he neared ever closer to Jerusalem, Jesus knew his time was approaching. Everyone seemed to have something negative to say about him or to him. In our time, we can see how media attention can affect those individuals who are in its crosshairs. Politicians and personalities alike can see their careers ended by the power of television and social media. Populist opinion can turn heroes into villains in the blink of an eye. The adulation of the crowd can give way to suspicion and anger. The Jews failed to understand what Jesus was speaking about. They got angry and wanted to stone him to death. Jesus did not alter his message in a bid to retain his popularity. He returned to a place of comfort, a place where people were less condemning. Sometimes we need to move out of the spotlight, to take stock during highly emotive situations. It is important to know where to go. We need to recognise that retreat and resignation are not synonymous; a retreat is the place where renewal and revival can happen. Jesus showed us that sometimes in the face of adversity – though it may seem contradictory – we need to step back in order to progress on our chosen path.

RESPOND

• When times are tough, where do you go on retreat? Is it a physical location or somewhere inside your heart?

• How do you step back from ridicule or rejection? Can you take some solace from Jesus and recognise that sometimes it is okay to step back?

SATURDAY

'And there Mary stands [at the foot of the cross], herself almost dead, but unfainting, unfaltering, offering her seed in the sacrifice … Christianity is not merely a belief. It is the practise of that belief by active charity.'

FRANK DUFF

'Forgiveness is never going to be easy. Each day it must be prayed for and struggled for and won.'

SR HELEN PREJEAN

READ

Today, slowly read the following passage from scripture and ponder each line carefully

My servant David shall be king over them; and they shall all have one shepherd. They shall follow my ordinances and be careful to observe my statutes. They shall live in the land that I gave to my servant Jacob, in which your ancestors lived; they and their children and their children's children shall live there for ever; and my servant David shall be their prince for ever. I will make a covenant of peace with them; it shall be an everlasting covenant with them; and I will bless them and multiply them and will set my sanctuary among them for evermore. My dwelling-place shall be with them; and I will be their God, and they shall be my people. Then the nations shall know that I the Lord sanctify Israel, when my sanctuary is among them for evermore. (Ez 37:24-28)

REFLECT

As we come closer to Holy Week, the scripture readings become more intense. People were seeking out Jesus for different reasons. Some were looking for Jesus in order to deepen their understanding of him. We hear about increasing numbers of people who were looking for Jesus just in case they were missing out on something. Jesus was acutely aware that not everyone who was curious about him had good intentions. Some were seeking out Jesus in order to curry favour with the establishment, effectively playing both sides. Jesus began to withdraw from public. He was very much aware that there were tensions. In testing times, we often return to a place of comfort or refuge. In order to prepare for difficult times ahead, it is good to build yourself up, to get strong in order to face the inevitable. Even though sometimes we know that we are facing into a difficult period in our life, we need to take solace that even Jesus did not go it alone. Even if you think the whole world is against you, surround yourself with people that matter or spend time in places that provide comfort. Know what side you are on. Are you the person who will seek out Jesus in an authentic manner? Or are you the person who will seek out Jesus as a kind of insurance policy when all else fails? To follow Jesus authentically requires total commitment. Jesus did not want weak followers. It is time to choose.

RESPOND

- How do you respond to the challenge of the Word of God?
- As you prepare to celebrate Holy Week, are you confident that you are ready to follow Christ totally with an open heart?

HOLY WEEK

PASSION (PALM) SUNDAY

'In the cross we discover what love really is. Love is not that we love God, but that God loved us first. Don't doubt God's love for you. The Father readily reveals himself to the lowly.'
POPE FRANCIS

'O most holy Cross, on which my Lord did hang, in deathly fear and pain. See how with spear and nails his every limb is torn, pierced are his hands and feet and side.'
TRADITIONAL GERMAN HYMN

'Jesus, for you I live; Jesus, for you I die; Jesus, I am yours in life and in death.'
CHURCH CHANT, AUGSBURG

'Hosanna to the Son of David, the King of Israel, Blessed is he who comes in the name of the Lord!'
ANTIPHON

'... for five weeks of Lent we have been preparing by works of charity and self-sacrifice, for the celebration of our Lord's paschal mystery. Today we come together to begin this solemn celebration ... Christ entered in triumph into his own city, to complete the work as our Messiah, to suffer, to die and to rise again.'
PALM SUNDAY INTRODUCTION

READ

Today, slowly read the following passage from scripture and ponder each line carefully
The disciples went and did as Jesus had directed them; they brought the donkey and the colt, and put their cloaks on them, and he sat on them. A very large crowd spread their cloaks on the road, and others cut branches from the trees and spread them on the road. The crowds that went ahead of him and that followed were shouting, 'Hosanna to the Son of David! Blessed is the one who comes in the name of the Lord! Hosanna in the highest heaven!' When he entered Jerusalem, the whole city was in turmoil, asking, 'Who is this?' The crowds were saying, 'This is the prophet Jesus from Nazareth in Galilee.' (Mt 21:6-11)

His state was divine, yet Christ Jesus did not cling to his equality with God but emptied himself to assume the condition of a slave ... He was humbler even to accepting death on a cross. (Phil 2:6-11)

REFLECT

Just days before the solemn Passover Jesus came to Jerusalem. There was major excitement with people cheering and singing. Adults and children welcomed Jesus to Jerusalem. They cried the blessed words of welcome and mercy. The cries would soon turn to jeers. Jesus did not set out to be popular. He was fully aware of the path he was on. The irony of being popular with those on the margins of Jerusalem is contrasted by his unpopularity with the elite of society in Jerusalem. The powerful would soon become powerless. Jesus complied, with full knowledge of the unfolding events. He knew what was to come. This Holy Week, no matter how you have participated in Lent, get yourself ready to be not merely a bystander, but someone who is part of the journey. The shadow of the cross permeates the readings. The drama of Holy Week is one that is familiar to Christians. This drama also requires us to enter the events and the story of how Jesus arrived in Jerusalem. In a way try to become part of the story. Try to identify with some of the key characters: the cheering crowds; those who plotted his downfall; Peter and his denials; the disciples; the women of Jerusalem who seemed to carry Jesus towards his cross and care for him after his death. Holy Week is full of emotions. Emotions are real. Holy Week is real. Prepare yourself to enter Holy Week paying close attention to the person of Jesus and the sacrifice that he made on our behalf.

RESPOND
- How do you plan to be part of Holy Week?
- Consider reading some of the scriptures before you attend one of the ceremonies.

MONDAY OF HOLY WEEK

*'Deep peace of the running wave to you; deep peace of
the flowing air to you; deep peace of the quiet earth to you;
deep peace of the shining stars to you; deep peace of the
son of peace to you.'*

IONA COMMUNITY

READ

Today, slowly read the following passage from scripture and ponder each line carefully

Six days before the Passover Jesus came to Bethany, the home of Lazarus, whom he had raised from the dead. There they gave a dinner for him. Martha served, and Lazarus was one of those at the table with him. Mary took a pound of costly perfume made of pure nard, anointed Jesus' feet, and wiped them with her hair. The house was filled with the fragrance of the perfume. But Judas Iscariot, one of his disciples (the one who was about to betray him), said, 'Why was this perfume not sold for three hundred denarii and the money given to the poor?' (He said this not because he cared about the poor, but because he was a thief; he kept the common purse and used to steal what was put into it.) Jesus said, 'Leave her alone. She bought it so that she might keep it for the day of my burial. You always have the poor with you, but you do not always have me.'

When the great crowd of the Jews learned that he was there, they came not only because of Jesus but also to see Lazarus, whom he had raised from the dead. So the chief priests planned to put Lazarus to death as well, since it was on account of him that many of the Jews were deserting and were believing in Jesus. (Jn 12:1-11)

REFLECT

Lazarus not only encountered Jesus once when he was brought back to life but continued this encounter. The initial zeal of any new relationship can peter out. Sometimes it must deepen or mature for the initial encounter to be sustained. Lazarus and Martha continue that deepening of their relationship with Jesus. We encounter Lazarus spending time with Jesus at the table. Martha also gave Jesus one of the most expensive ointments. There are shadows of what is to come later this Holy Week. There is an echo of 'supper', a communal meal and the 'anointing' of Jesus. Our initial encounter with Jesus will not bear fruit unless we are prepared to spend quality time with him. To continue this encounter involves serving at the feet of Jesus as Martha did. We are told in the Gospel that the Jews wanted to see Jesus but also see Lazarus for themselves. Sometimes people may encounter Jesus first through another person. All our actions can provide a signpost to others in pointing towards Jesus. On the road to Jerusalem this week the characters we will encounter are all pointing towards Jesus.

RESPOND

• When people look at us, do they see signposts pointing towards Jesus?

• How have you deepened your relationship with Jesus during these weeks of Lent? Have you noticed a difference?

• How can you continue it beyond Easter Sunday?

• In your life, do you relate more to Martha or Mary – are you too busy preparing for Jesus to actually spend quality time with him?

TUESDAY OF HOLY WEEK
*'False witnesses have stood up against me, and my enemies
threaten violence; Lord, do not surrender me into their power!'*
ENTRANCE ANTIPHON

READ
Today, slowly read the following passage from scripture and ponder each line carefully
Simon Peter said to him, 'Lord, where are you going?' Jesus
answered, 'Where I am going, you cannot follow me now;
but you will follow afterwards.' Peter said to him, 'Lord, why
can I not follow you now? I will lay down my life for you.'
Jesus answered, 'Will you lay down your life for me? Very
truly, I tell you, before the cock crows, you will have denied
me three times.' (Jn 13:36-38)

REFLECT
Many people view the world through the prism of reality
television, social media and the gossip pages. Sometimes there
is a cost to fame and notoriety. Just as some of these celebrities
are made famous, the mechanism that created their 'fame' can
also destroy them. Many of the 'idols' of music, TV, politics
and even of the Church can find it hard to cope when they
fall from public view. They can struggle once the adoration
has been replaced with indifference. There is a cost to fame.
Jesus also hinted at that in John's Gospel when he implied to
Peter that there was a cost to discipleship. Peter would learn
this the hard way. He tried to be brave when he pledged his
support to Jesus. Jesus rebuked him and said that even as a
'follower' he would also deny Jesus. Jesus was certainly on a
pedestal for Peter and the disciples. Jesus reminded them that

following him came with a cost. Jesus was not a hero or an idol. For the disciples they would learn the truth in time that being attracted to the fame of Jesus was not enough. Jesus was preparing them for a new chapter in the relationship with him. It is not just enough to be close to Jesus and to say the right things to him. Jesus is asking the disciples for a different kind of loyalty. There is a cost to being a disciple. The disciples would soon learn this lesson.

RESPOND

• Are there times that you may have 'denied' your relationship with Jesus, because it was easier than justifying your relationship with him? We pray that in these moments of weakness we can take strength that Jesus' plan is bigger than ours.

• Who are the people that you look up to? Are you really a follower of them? What do you learn from them?

WEDNESDAY OF HOLY WEEK

*'When I survey the wondrous cross on which the Prince of
Glory died; my richest gain I count but loss,
and pour contempt on all my pride.'*

TRADITIONAL HYMN

*'You cannot understand Christianity without understanding
this profound humiliation of the Son of God who humbled
himself and became a servant unto death, even death on a cross,
in order to save us.'*

POPE FRANCIS

READ

Today, slowly read the following passage from scripture and ponder each line carefully

On the first day of Unleavened Bread the disciples came to Jesus, saying, 'Where do you want us to make the preparations for you to eat the Passover?' He said, 'Go into the city to a certain man, and say to him, "The Teacher says, My time is near; I will keep the Passover at your house with my disciples."' So the disciples did as Jesus had directed them, and they prepared the Passover meal.

When it was evening, he took his place with the twelve; and while they were eating, he said, 'Truly I tell you, one of you will betray me.' And they became greatly distressed and began to say to him one after another, 'Surely not I, Lord?' He answered, 'The one who has dipped his hand into the bowl with me will betray me. The Son of Man goes as it is written of him, but woe to that one by whom the Son of Man is betrayed! It would have been better for that one not to have been born.' Judas, who betrayed him, said, 'Surely not I, Rabbi?' He replied, 'You have said so.' (Mt 26:14-25)

REFLECT

The readings for today still have Jesus in Bethany. There is a lot going on. There are rumours of plots unfolding to get rid of Jesus. Some of the disciples get annoyed with Martha 'wasting' precious ointment on Jesus that could have been sold to raise money for the poor. We encounter Judas the apostle who planned to hand Jesus over to the authorities for money. Judas had gone over to the other side. His betrayal of Jesus was complete. When Jesus hinted at his betrayal Judas spoke the words 'surely not I'. Jesus knew his accuser. He knew the fate that was ahead of him. Darkness had entered Judas. Judas had become the spy, the deceiver. Jesus was the 'light of the world' and here he is in his Tenebrae moment of facing the darkness in someone very close to him. Jesus knew his betrayer very well. Many of us have encountered people who have betrayed us. Some of these people are usually very close to us. It is hurtful and hard to fathom. We are all faced with moments of temptation or weakness where it might be easy to 'take the money' rather than act with integrity. It is very easy to become Judas. It is harder to become like Jesus. Each of us needs to look at the areas of darkness in our lives and choose to follow the light, rather than risk uttering the words: 'not I'.

RESPOND

• How do you react if you are deceived in any way?
• Many people experience periods of darkness. If you notice someone who is 'not themselves', reach out to them with kindness.

HOLY THURSDAY

'The Eucharist is a precious nourishment for faith: an encounter with Christ truly present in the supreme act of his love, the life-giving gift of himself.'

POPE FRANCIS

'...we are gathered here to share in the supper which your only Son left to his Church to reveal his love. He gave it to us when he was about to die and commanded us to celebrate it as the new and eternal sacrifice.'

OPENING PRAYER

READ

Today, slowly read the following passage from scripture and ponder each line carefully
For I received from the Lord what I also handed on to you, that the Lord Jesus on the night when he was betrayed took a loaf of bread, and when he had given thanks, he broke it and said, 'This is my body that is for you. Do this in remembrance of me.' In the same way he took the cup also, after supper, saying, 'This cup is the new covenant in my blood. Do this, as often as you drink it, in remembrance of me.' For as often as you eat this bread and drink the cup, you proclaim the Lord's death until he comes. (1 Cor 11:23-36)

REFLECT

In some organisations, managers take on the duties of those on a lower pay grade in order to fully understand the role. It comes from the theory of never asking someone to do a job if you are not prepared to do it yourself. In a way, it is a type of servant leadership. Jesus was a leader who not only used words and symbolism but also left a legacy of actions. What we call the Last Supper contains words, ritual and actions that will be remembered right up to this day. He took on the form of a servant and demonstrated what being a disciple is all about. The washing of the feet, the meal in common brought together key actions that Jesus wanted the disciples to continue later.

If we belong to Christ, we must follow his example of self-giving and service. To wash another's feet is an act of humility and grace. The challenge to each of us during these days of the Easter Triduum is to reflect on how much of Jesus' legacy we can continue in our personal life. Can we become like Christ and say 'this is my body given up for you?' In the face of what is to come, our faith needs to take inspiration from Jesus. He knew the outcome of the days ahead. He also remained faithful in the adversity that was to come. There are days in our life when we will have our last meal, meet our friends for one last time knowing that things are going to change. Whatever Calvary awaits any one of us, Jesus shows us how the servant model of humility is also a model of strength. After the crucifixion, it was these moments of Jesus' last words and actions that became pivotal and inspirational for the disciples. We can take hope that when we 'empty ourselves' we find our greatest strength.

RESPOND

• Consider planning a family meal, just to celebrate family and faith.

• What actions of humility do you occasionally carry out? How have you washed the feet of others?

GOOD FRIDAY

'But what exactly does Jesus' death accomplish? For John, Good Friday is already Pentecost. On the one hand, Jesus hands his life over to God, from whom he received it. But he also hands it over to his disciples. Even the bowing of his head at the moment of death can be interpreted as a nod in their direction. Out of Jesus' death comes life for his followers. In colloquial speech today, Jesus might have said, "Mission accomplished!" It's in your hands now!'

FR TOM ROSICA

'As he said, blessed are they who are not scandalised by his cross. Lent thus is a call to celebrate our redemption in that difficult combination of cross and victory. Our people are well prepared to do so these days; all our environment proclaims the cross. But those who have Christian faith and hope know that behind this Calvary of El Salvador lies our Easter, our Resurrection. This is the Christian people's hope.'

ÓSCAR ROMERO

READ

So they took Jesus; and carrying the cross by himself, he went out to what is called The Place of the Skull, which in Hebrew is called Golgotha. There they crucified him, and with him two others, one on either side, with Jesus between them. Pilate also had an inscription written and put on the cross. It read, 'Jesus of Nazareth, the King of the Jews.' Many of the Jews read this inscription, because the place where Jesus was crucified was near the city; and it was written in Hebrew, in

Latin, and in Greek. Then the chief priests of the Jews said to Pilate, 'Do not write, "The King of the Jews", but, "This man said, I am King of the Jews." ' Pilate answered, 'What I have written I have written.' When the soldiers had crucified Jesus, they took his clothes and divided them into four parts, one for each soldier. They also took his tunic; now the tunic was seamless, woven in one piece from the top. So they said to one another, 'Let us not tear it, but cast lots for it to see who will get it.' This was to fulfil what the scripture says, 'They divided my clothes among themselves, and for my clothing they cast lots.' And that is what the soldiers did.

Meanwhile, standing near the cross of Jesus were his mother, and his mother's sister, Mary the wife of Clopas, and Mary Magdalene. When Jesus saw his mother and the disciple whom he loved standing beside her, he said to his mother, 'Woman, here is your son.' Then he said to the disciple, 'Here is your mother.' And from that hour the disciple took her into his own home.

After this, when Jesus knew that all was now finished, he said (in order to fulfil the scripture), 'I am thirsty.' A jar full of sour wine was standing there. So they put a sponge full of the wine on a branch of hyssop and held it to his mouth. When Jesus had received the wine, he said, 'It is finished.' Then he bowed his head and gave up his spirit. (Jn 19:17-30)

REFLECT

There is a stillness and starkness to Good Friday. The shadow of the cross on the horizon becomes real to us. As we listen to the word of God on the day, we know that Jesus 'knew it was complete'. It had to be this way. Jesus needed to die. It was necessary for all to have a whole new relationship with God.

The cross is not just a cultural symbol. The cross is something that each one of us needs to appreciate. In order to have a continued relationship with Jesus, we need to remember that Jesus went through all of this for each of us. The cross is a personal reminder of how we deepen in our understanding of faith and relationship. It is part of the memorial of faith. The cross brings us further on the path to new life because of the triumphant death and Resurrection of Jesus. The cross brought closure to some people who wanted Jesus gone. However, the cross brings hope. We notice those who found a new strength to help Jesus on his way to the cross. We have met Veronica, Simon and Joseph who try to help Jesus. Each of us can reach out to help another person in their darkest hours. Jesus was merciful until the end, offering paradise to the sinner on the cross next to him because he was able to recognise that Jesus offered something different. On this Good Friday, as you notice the world which seems at one remove from the example of Jesus, it is our duty to remind the world that Jesus' humility on the cross was not an act of failure but of heroism. The personal crosses that we carry at some point can be turned into hope. Our darkest hour will pass. This is part of the mystery of the cross: knowing when to relinquish our burden and pass it over to God.

RESPOND

• Take some time to look at the cross and reflect on what Jesus has done for you and take time to give thanks for this selfless action.

• Does your home have a cross on the wall? Maybe invest in one as a simple reminder of your faith.

HOLY SATURDAY

'On this most holy night, when our Lord Jesus Christ
passed from death to life, the Church invites her children
throughout the world to come together in vigil and prayer.
This is the Passover of the Lord: if we honour the memory
of his death and Resurrection by hearing his word and
celebrating his mysteries, then we may be confident that
we shall share his victory over death.'

GREETING AT THE VIGIL LITURGY

'This is the night when Christians everywhere, washed clean of
sin and freed from all defilement, are restored to grace and grow
together in holiness. This is the night when Jesus Christ broke
the chains of death and rose triumphant from the grave.'

GAUDETE ET EXSULATE

READ

After the sabbath, as the first day of the week was dawning,
Mary Magdalene and the other Mary went to see the tomb.
And suddenly there was a great earthquake; for an angel of
the Lord, descending from heaven, came and rolled back the
stone and sat on it. His appearance was like lightning, and his
clothing white as snow. For fear of him the guards shook and
became like dead men. But the angel said to the women, 'Do
not be afraid; I know that you are looking for Jesus who was
crucified. He is not here; for he has been raised, as he said.
Come, see the place where he lay. Then go quickly and tell his
disciples, "He has been raised from the dead, and indeed he is

going ahead of you to Galilee; there you will see him." This is my message for you.' So they left the tomb quickly with fear and great joy, and ran to tell his disciples. Suddenly Jesus met them and said, 'Greetings!' And they came to him, took hold of his feet, and worshipped him. Then Jesus said to them, 'Do not be afraid; go and tell my brothers to go to Galilee; there they will see me.' (Mt 28:1-10)

REFLECT

Holy Saturday is a day of waiting. It is a day of reflection, as we await the return of the Lord and meditate on his suffering and death. Churches are left bare. As we move towards the solemn vigil which begins in darkness, we begin to sense the anticipation of the Resurrection. Holy Saturday is a night filled with ritual. The readings for this night echo the ancient tradition of waiting for the Lord. The gap in our life is bridged by God's gift to us, namely, his Son. Luke's Gospel reminds us to have our lamps burning brightly for that moment when the 'master' returns to the table. Gradually, our reflections turn towards our Baptism. The anticipation of the Resurrection also echoes how all the faithful, the baptised, are reborn in Baptism. Reciting our baptismal promises can be a recommitment to stay on the journey of faith. The shadow of the cross is still present. However, there is a new light and it can hold our attention. As we gather around the eucharistic table on this night, we are now connected to and part of God's plan. God's revelation to the world is also a revelation to each of us to repeatedly enter his invitation to follow him. This encounter with the Lord will lead us through many experiences. We are not alone. The Lord has prepared a way for each of us because of his passion, death and Resurrection. Holy Saturday is a day of contemplation on the Pascal Mystery, the mystery that God has a plan for each of us. Our relationship with him is a journey of enrichment from our Baptism right through to the end of our lives. The newness of life in God continues. The story has not ended. The cross becomes a shadow pointing towards hope.

RESPOND

• This evening why not repeat this line: 'Christ has died, Christ is risen, Christ will come again.'

• Greet people you meet and wish them a Happy Easter – and smile as you say it!

EASTER SUNDAY

'Thine be the glory, risen, conqu'ring Son; endless is the victory,
thou o'er death hast won; angels in bright raiment rolled the
stone away, kept the folded grave clothes where thy body lay.
Thine is the glory, risen conqu'ring son, endless is the vict'ry,
thou o'er death hast won.'

EASTER HYMN

'Easter is itself now the cry of victory. No one can quench
that life that Christ has resurrected. Neither death nor all the
banners of death and hatred raised against him and against his
Church can prevail. He is the victorious one.'

ÓSCAR ROMERO

'Christ has become our paschal sacrifice; let us feast with the
unleavened bread of sincerity and truth.'

COMMUNION ANTIPHON

READ

Today, slowly read the following passage from scripture and ponder each line carefully

Early on the first day of the week, while it was still dark, Mary
Magdalene came to the tomb and saw that the stone had been
removed from the tomb. So she ran and went to Simon Peter
and the other disciple, the one whom Jesus loved, and said
to them, 'They have taken the Lord out of the tomb, and we
do not know where they have laid him.' Then Peter and the
other disciple set out and went towards the tomb. The two
were running together, but the other disciple outran Peter
and reached the tomb first. He bent down to look in and saw

the linen wrappings lying there, but he did not go in. Then Simon Peter came, following him, and went into the tomb. He saw the linen wrappings lying there, and the cloth that had been on Jesus' head, not lying with the linen wrappings but rolled up in a place by itself. Then the other disciple, who reached the tomb first, also went in, and he saw and believed; for as yet they did not understand the scripture, that he must rise from the dead. (Jn 20:1-9)

REFLECT

Certainty and belief do not necessarily go hand in hand. Some people grow in their faith and trust in God. Our Christian history is full of great people who came to faith as a result of an unexpected encounter or episode. On the first day of the Resurrection, John's Gospel shows us how Peter, on hearing the news that Jesus was not in the tomb, entered and then believed. Finally, all his encounters with Jesus and all the stories that he heard fell into place. He finally understood that everything that Jesus had said was true. The impossible was now possible. Jesus had risen from the dead. Unbelievable as it sounds, it was true. Everything that had happened with Peter and Jesus now took on a new perspective. Peter didn't change, but a change had occurred in him. A new authority and a new motivation to tell people that Jesus is alive took place. Peter, who had denied Jesus, now became the person charged with providing an eye-witness account – at any cost. Just like Peter we are witnesses to something amazing. Our faith is one of hope and rooted in the personal relationship we have with Jesus who endured everything out of love for each of us. Jesus saved us by being on this earth; on the cross and through the sacrifice of love he has given us a new hope and a new relationship with God. Nothing can separate us from God anymore. Lent leads to Easter. Our life can have a new focus with Jesus at the centre of it. His way is a new way. Jesus is risen and this is the certainty we need for our belief. To God everything is possible.

RESPOND

• If you have walked the path of Lent and arrived at Easter Sunday, what have you learned about yourself and your relationship with Jesus Christ?

• As a Christian, how do you bring your Easter joy to other people and in the circumstances that you find yourself?

• Is your life an Alleluia? Or, do you live your life as an Alleluia?

Leabharlann Contae na Mídhe

123

BIBLIOGRAPHY

- Scripture quotations taken from the New Revised Standard Version Bible (Oremus).
- Additional scripture quotations from The Jerusalem Bible, popular edition, London: Darton, Longman & Todd, 1974.
- Papal quotations from *The Holy See*, www.vatican.va.
- Catechism of the Catholic Church, Geoffrey Chapman, London, 1994.
- *DOCAT: The Social Teaching of the Catholic Church*, San Francisco: Ignatius Press, 2016.
- *Documents of Vatican II*, London: Geoffrey Chapman, London, 1966.
- *Hymns Old and New*, London: Kevin Mayhew, 1989.
- *Westminster Hymnal*, London: Burns, Oates & Washbourne, 1948.
- *YOUCAT: Youth Catechism of the Catholic Church*, San Francisco: Ignatius Press, 2010.
- *YOUCAT: Youth Prayer Book*, San Francisco: Ignatius Press, 2011.
- Bourke, E., *Mercy in All Things: Reflections on the Diary of St Faustina Kowalska*, Dublin: Veritas, 2019.
- Coote, T., *Live While You Can: A Memoir of Faith*, Dublin: Hachette Books Ireland, 2019.
- Ferrer Blehl, V., *John Henry Newman 1901–1890*, Newman Secretariat, 1991.
- Pope Francis, *Christus Vivit*, Dublin: Veritas, 2019.
- ——, *Laudato Si'*, Dublin: Veritas, 2015.
- ——, *Gaudete et Exultate*, Dublin: Veritas, 2018.
- ——, *Evangelii Gaudium*, Dublin: Veritas, 2013.
- Midgley, JB, *Lent with the Saints: Sayings and Meditations*, London: CTS, 2006.

- O'Donohue, J., *Anam Cara: Spiritual Wisdom from the Celtic World*, London: Bantam Press, 1997.
- Romero, Óscar, *The Violence of Love: The Pastoral Wisdom of Archbishop Óscar Romero*, New York: Harper & Row, 1988.
- Rosica, T., *The Seven Last Words of Christ: Reflections by Thomas Rosica*, New London: Twenty-Third Publications, 2017.
- Travers, A., *Oxygen for the Soul: Prayers and Reflections for Teenagers*, Dublin: Veritas, 2015.
- Vandeleene, M. (ed.), *Chiara Lubich: Essential Writings*, New York: New City Press, 2007.
- Van Dyke, M., *Radical Integrity: The Story of Dietrich Bonhoeffer*, Ohio: Barbour Publishing, 2001.
- Ward, H. and J. Wild, *Christian Quotations and Meditations*, Oxford: Lion Books, 1998.

This journey through Lent will follow the readings of Year A, but it can also be read during years B and C. Please note that certain feasts take place during Lent: St Patrick's Day, 17 March; St Joseph, 19 March; The Annunciation, 25 March. These feasts are echoed in some of the reflections during the Season of Lent.